COMPUTE!'s
Advanced
Turbo C™
Programming

Steve Burnap

COMPUTE! Books

Greensboro, North Carolina
Radnor, Pennsylvania

Printed in the United States of America

10 9 8 7 6 5 4 3 2 1

Library of Congress Cataloging-in-Publication Data

Burnap, Steve.
    Compute!'s advanced Turbo C programming / Steve Burnap.
        p. cm.
    On t.p. the registered trademark symbol "TM" is superscript
    following "C" in the title.
    Includes index.
    ISBN 0-87455-151-X :
    1. C (Computer program language) 2. Turbo C (Computer program)
    I. Compute! Publications, Inc. II. Title.
QA76.73.C15B88 1988
005.13'3--dc19   88-22858
                                                           CIP

COMPUTE! Books, Post Office Box 5406, Greensboro, North Carolina 27403, (919) 275-9809, is a Capital Cities/ABC, Inc. company and is not associated with any manufacturer of personal computers. Turbo C is a trademark of Borland International, Inc. IBM is a registered trademark of International Business Machines Corporation.

Contents

Appendices

Foreword

COMPUTE!'s *Advanced Turbo C Programming* is the easy-to-use advanced programming guide for *Turbo C* on your IBM PC, PC XT, PC AT, or compatible. Although it contains advanced programming examples, this book assumes only that you're familiar with another language, whether that language is C, Pascal, assembly language, or BASIC.

COMPUTE!'s *Advanced Turbo C Programming* progresses rapidly from the rudiments, like declaring variables and using operators, to advanced topics, such as using interrupts, graphics, and writing hot-key programs that lie dormant in memory until you need them.
mm*Turbo C* from Borland International is quickly establishing itself as a standard against which all other versions of C are judged. It's flexible and powerful, fast and friendly. *COMPUTE!'s Advanced Turbo C Programming* will win you over to programming in C. Learn how to use IBM internals and interrupts in your C programs. You'll also learn how graphics are used and much more.

This book has it all. Chapter 3 covers the basic structure of a C program. Chapters 5 and 6 show you how to use conditional operators and math. By Chapters 25 and 26, you'll be using the clock and keyboard interrupts. In the final chapters, you'll learn about graphics and the debugger, a unique feature of *Turbo C* that makes the language especially friendly and useful. Finally, you'll find information-packed appendices.

Written in everyday language and advancing through *Turbo C* in easy steps, COMPUTE!'s *Advanced Turbo C Programming* is the book you need to get moving with *Turbo C*.

Chapter 1

Introduction

Yet another *Turbo C* book.

There are a score of standard C texts on the market and even a number of books on *Turbo C*. Why was this book written? Does the world really need another C programming manual?

Learning to use *Turbo C* on the IBM PC proved to be a frustrating experience. The language itself was easy enough. Once you've learned one or two languages, you'll pick up others easily. It was the details of the PC architecture that eluded me.

There were many books available concerning the basics of C. I didn't want the basics, though; I wanted the details. I wanted to write programs that used the machine to its full potential. Learning how to use loops and arrays is all well and good, but I certainly didn't need a book that spent 50 pages on the subject. A short description of how loops are used in *Turbo C* was all I really needed.

There are a number of good books that will show you some of the lower-level details of the IBM PC. Most books nearly always use BASIC or machine language. Unfortunately, machine language didn't offer the high level I required, and BASIC offers neither the speed nor flexibility I needed.

Most books were far too simple *(The on switch is located on the right side of the machine, near the back)* or were very hard to read *(To reset vectors used by the 8519a, use DOS function 31h while ensuring that routines that may be called multiple times are made reentrant)*. I didn't want to waste my time wading through a text meant for novices, and I didn't want to waste my time reading a book written in "programmerese." All I wanted was a book to tell me—in English—how to use the IBM PC to its full potential through *Turbo C*.

The *Turbo C* manuals themselves were helpful in many respects. But the *Turbo C* manuals spend most of their resources on details directly related to that version of the language. It isn't their job to explain the pitfalls of direct memory access or of accessing the BIOS routines.

I was forced to read a number of manuals, using experiments to discover by trial and error how everything fits together. While I did find a number of good books, no single book had all of the information I wanted. A few books came close, but they used machine language. Writing similar routines in C was often an entirely different problem. I had to take the information I had learned and experiment with it until I was able to develop routines that worked in C.

This book contains what I've learned. This is the book that I would have liked to read one year ago.

You don't need to know C to use this book. It assumes any potential reader knows the basics of programming. If you know about loops and arrays and variables, this book shouldn't prove too difficult for you. Because there's a great deal of information to cover, the basics of the language are presented very quickly. For example, while this book gives complete information on how arrays are used in C, it doesn't stop to explain what an array is. This book wasn't intended to be your first exposure to programming, though it could do well as your second exposure if you're already familiar with BASIC, Pascal, or any other programming language.

Much of this book is concerned not with how the C language works but how it can be used to perform certain tasks. For instance, you'll see how to use the screen in the most efficient manner, how to create pop-up programs, and how to write programs that run in the background while other programs are running also. These are some of the techniques I wanted to learn. Now that I've invested the time to learn the techniques, I'll share them with you.

But why use C at all? All of the things I'll show you can be done with machine language. Why is C better?

C, like Pascal or BASIC, is a high-level language. High-level languages are always converted to machine language before they're executed. A single C statement may be converted to a great number of machine language instructions. When you write in machine language, you find yourself rewriting simple routines to perform mundane tasks like printing to the screen or reading from the keyboard.

In the past, programmers resorted to machine language for two reasons: To gain the speed of machine language or to access the internals of the IBM PC more easily. *Turbo C* is nearly as fast as machine language and can access all of the internals of the IBM PC. So why use machine language when you can keep all the power and have the advantages of a high-level language at the same time? *Turbo C* provides all the utility you should ever need.

Chapter 2
Using *Turbo C*

A computer program can be either interpreted or compiled. If it's interpreted, programs must be loaded into a separate program called an interpreter. The interpreter reads a statement from the program, translates it into machine language, and then executes the machine language translation. It then gets the next statement in the program and repeats the translation-execution process for it.

When a computer program is compiled, it is read by a program called a compiler. The compiler translates the whole program into a machine language—executable file. This file can be run independently of any other program. A compiled program runs much faster than when it's interpreted.

Turbo C is a C compiler. There are actually two separate compilers included with *Turbo C*. The integrated *Turbo C* environment comprises a complete program-development system including a compiler and editor. Also included is a more traditional compiler, which can be run from the command line. Both compilers produce the same code.

The *Turbo C* command line compiler is the simplest to describe. The command TCC invokes the C compiler to translate any files listed on the command line. Thus the command TCC TEST.C would compile the program test.c and produce the executable file TEST.EXE. If the program is made up of a number of files, they all must be listed on the command line: TCC TEST.C TEST1.C TEST2.C

TCC will accept any standard C file whose filename ends with .C. If you give TCC a filename that doesn't end in .C, *Turbo C* will automatically append the .C for you. How you create the program text is completely up to you. You can use any program editor or word processor that produces straight ASCII text files (such as *WordStar* in nondocument mode). You can even use the *Turbo C* editor to create the file. All files are completely cross-compatible between TCC and TC. They're really the same compiler with different packaging.

The integrated *Turbo C* environment provides all the features necessary to produce C programs including a compiler, editor, and file handler. The integrated environment is invoked with TC. When you type *TC* at the DOS prompt, you'll be placed in the integrated environment. To create a program, simply choose EDIT from the main menu at the top of the screen. You'll be placed in a *WordStar*-like editor in which you may create your program. The Run option from the main menu allows you to execute your program, first compiling it, if necessary. The File option allows you to save and load programs. It's important to remember that even if you have compiled and run a program many times from within the environment, it won't be saved to disk unless you explicitly save it through the File options.

Many *Turbo C* functions have been assigned to function keys as well as menu options. These keys are available from anywhere within the environment. In this way, you can avoid moving through the menus. Figure 2-1 contains a list of often-used keys.

Figure 2-1. A List of Frequently Used Keys

Key	Action
Alt-E	Enters the editor
Alt-R	Runs program, compiling if necessary
Alt-X	Leaves integrated environment
Alt-C	Takes you to the compiler menu
F1	Help
F2	Save the program
F3	Load a program
F10	Main menu

These keys will appear next to the command with which they're associated in any of the pull-down menus. Additional function key commands will appear on the bottom line of the environment. These commands are specific to the current portion of the environment.

When compiling, the integrated environment keeps track of any errors found in the program and remembers them as you return to the editor. You can move quickly to all lines with errors from within the environment. This greatly speeds the debugging process. On the other hand, when you use the command line environment, you must remember the errors and the lines on which they occurred as you modify them in your favorite editor.

You'll find that the environment is very easy to use. It tends to compile faster than the command line compiler as it keeps as much of the program in memory as possible.

The only disadvantages to using the environment exclusively are that you can't use your favorite editor and you can't use in-line machine language. In-line machine language should be avoided as much as possible, anyway. It's fairly easy to modify the *Turbo C* editor commands to suit a person's tastes. For this reason, most people will want to use the environment. Most of the examples were written in the environment with the exception of a few memory-resident programs.

Turbo C also includes a number of other programs as well as TC and TCC. TLINK is used to combine multiple object files together into a single executable file. Because TCC uses TLINK for exactly this purpose, there is rarely a need to use this command on its own.

Turbo C also includes a macro preprocessor in a file called CPP. This program is usually only used in debugging macros and will be described more fully in Chapter 7.

MAKE is a project-management facility for the command line compiler. It allows you to manage multiple program text files easily. Once the *makefile* has been created, you may compile your program simply by typing *MAKE. Turbo C* will recompile only those files that have been modified. There is a similar feature in the integrated environment called the *project*.

TOUCH is used in conjunction with MAKE. It marks a file as modified without actually changing the program, forcing MAKE to recompile the file.

TCINST allows you to modify the way the integrated environment works. You may change such things as the colors the editor displays as well as the command keys used by the editor.

Chapter 3
The Basic Structure of a C Program

The basic unit in a C program is a *statement*. A statement is a single action. C separates statements with a semicolon (;). More than one statement may appear on a single line, and statements may cover more than a single line.

One or more statements can be grouped together into a larger unit called a *block*. A block is delimited by braces ({ }) and may contain any number of statements or blocks. All statements in the block must be completely within the braces.

A block is also considered a legal statement. Thus blocks may contain other blocks. This is called *nesting* of blocks.

A program is made up of a number of *functions*. Each function contains one block (which may contain other blocks). A function may never contain another function. The different functions that make up a program may be spread between text files though each function must occupy one file only. Every program must have at least one function called *main ( )*.

Programs may also include compiler directives and comments. Compiler directives aren't part of the program itself but actually are used by the compiler to determine how the program is compiled. Compiler directives begin with a pound sign (#).

Comments are notes made by the programmer that don't affect the program in any way. They may appear at any point in the program and are surrounded by the symbols /* and */. Any characters between these two symbols are ignored completely.

Figure 3-1 contains a short example program containing all of these features. It's included to give you a feel for the way a C program looks.

Figure 3-1. Sample C Program

```
/* This is a comment at the beginning of the program */
#include <stdio.h> /* A compiler directive */

main() /* This is a function */
{ /* The beginning of block 1 */
  int i=0,j;

  printf("Hit 'q' to quit\n"); /* A statement */

  for(;getch() != 'q';printf("Hit 'q' to quit\n"))
    { /* The beginning of block 2 */
      /* Nested inside block 1 */

      i++; j = i+9;   /* 2 statements */
      printf("Looped statement # %d\n",j-9);

    } /* The end of block 2 */

} /* The end of block 1 */
```

Don't feel that you have to understand what each of these statements does. This example is just meant to give you a feel for the way a C program is put together. This program doesn't actually do anything useful. In the next few chapters, you'll learn how C functions build upon this basic structure.

Chapter 4

Variables and Data Types

Most programming languages use variables of some sort or
other. C is no exception. Languages create variables in one of
two different ways. Less-structured languages like BASIC or
Fortran tend to allow implicit declaration of variables. To create a variable, you simply use it in a command. In other languages such as Pascal or C, you must explicitly declare the
type of each variable before it's used.

Nearly all languages use the same three basic variable
types. Variables can hold whole numbers, real numbers, or
characters. In C, variables of type *float* hold real numbers,
variables of type *int* hold integers, and variables of type *char*
hold characters. To declare a variable or set of variables, you
specify a type followed by a list of variables separated by
commas. For instance, the following line would declare three
integer variables with the names *a1, a2,* and *a3:*

int a1,a2,a3;

As with any C statement, the variable declaration must
be terminated with a semicolon.

Every variable must be declared before it can be used.
Variable declarations must come before any executable statements in a block. In addition, you may declare each variable
only once in a given block. Variables may be used only in
the block in which they're declared. Consider the set of
blocks in Figure 4-1.

Figure 4-1. Declaring Variables

```
{
/* block 1 */
char a,b,c;
int x,y;
}

{
/* block 2 */
char c;
int a,x,z;
}

{
/* block 3 */
char another;
}
```

Each of these blocks has its own set of variables. They're completely independent of each other and can only be used in the block in which they're declared. Variable *y*, for example, could only be used in statements in block 1. Statements in block 1 and block 2 could both access a variable called *c*.

Note that the variable *c* in block 1 and the variable *c* in block 2 are completely different variables. Variables are always only accessible from the block in which they're declared, for all purposes. Thus the declaration of *c* in block 2 isn't a redeclaration of a variable but a declaration of entirely new variable. Note that the variable *a* seems to have two different types: char in block 1 and int in block 2. This is possible only because these are two different variables.

Because a block may contain other blocks, the rules for variable use can become tricky. Normally a variable may only be declared once in each block, however a new variable with the same name can be declared in a sub-block of that block. In such a case, this new variable supersedes the older one for that sub-block only. For example, consider the block in Figure 4-2.

Figure 4-2. Declaring Variables in Sub-Blocks

```
{
/* block 1 */
  char a,b,c;
  {
  /* block 1.1 */
    int a;
    /* A statement */
      a = 44;
  }

a = 'a';

{
/* block 1.2 */
  /* Some statements */
  }
}
```

Normally when a statement in block 1 uses the variable *a,* it will use the first declaration – char. If, however, that statement is in block 1.1, the integer variable *a* will be used instead. As before, these two *a*'s are completely separate variables. They have no connection other than their name. Also, because of the identical names, there is no way to access the character variable *a* from inside block 1.1 though this variable could be accessed from blocks 1 and 1.2.

When C sees a variable in an executable statement, it first looks for the declaration in the most local block (the block containing the statement). If the declaration isn't found, it then looks in the next outer block. If the variable still isn't found, it continues moving outward until the variable is found. Note that the entire program is considered to be a single block. Thus variables declared outside of any block boundaries are considered to belong to the program as a whole and may be used anywhere from within the program. These are called *global variables.*

You may assign values to a variable as it's declared. This is done simply by setting it equal to a value from within the variable declaration. For example, the following would declare the variables *a, b,* and *c,* setting them equal to 1, 2, and 3, respectively:

int a = 1,b = 2,c = 3;

In order to assign noninteger values, you need to know how to write values of each of the various types. As you can see from the previous example, any number without a decimal point is considered to be an integer. Not surprisingly, any number with a decimal point, even if it's a whole number, is considered to be a floating-point (real) number. Characters are written as any single character enclosed in single quotation marks (' ').

ints	floats	chars
1	2.3	'f'
− 525	4.341	'F'
− 4124	− 54.23	'%'
99	9.0	'{'

In addition, integers can be written in hexadecimal (base 16) and octal (base 8) as well as decimal. Octal constants have a leading 0. Hexadecimal constants have a leading 0 followed by an *x*. Letters in hexadecimal digits may be either upper- or lowercase.

hexadecimal ints	octal ints
0x43	045
0xff	01777
0xFDEA	03743
0x00	0100

It's important to remember that, because of this convention, the constant 055 isn't equal to the constant 55. The first constant is octal 55 (decimal 45), while the second is decimal 55. Only use a leading 0 with octal numbers.

The type-sensitivity of a language can range from the very type-sensitive, in which values of different types can never be intermixed, to the very type-insensitive, in which types can be mixed freely. C is a relatively type-insensitive language. You can often assign values of one type to another. The type of that value will automatically be converted to the type of the variable.

Values are assigned to a variable in a program just as they were in a declaration. The value on the right side of the equal sign must have the same type as the variable on the left side. In many cases, you don't need to worry about this because C will automatically convert the value on the right side to the appropriate type before it's assigned to the variable on the left side.

Consider the statements in Figure 4-3.

Figure 4-3. Assigning Values to a Variable of the Type Int

```
int a;
a = 5;
a = 4.5;
a = 'f';
```

All three assignments in Figure 4-3 are legal. In the first case, the value of 5 is assigned to *a*. In the second case, 4.5 is assigned to *a*. Because 4.5 is not an integer, it's truncated to the number 4 before it's assigned to *a*. In the last case, you'll note that the character *f* isn't an integer. However, each character has a number associated with it called its *ASCII value*. The character *f* is replaced with its ASCII value of 102, which is an integer. This value is then assigned to the variable *a*.

Note that while C always makes these conversions, it isn't always successful. The different types have different sizes in memory and thus can hold different ranges of numbers. There are floats, for example, that are too large to fit into an int. In addition, there are integers that are too large to be legal characters. In most cases, C won't consider it an error when you attempt to stuff a large number into a small variable. Instead, it will attempt to convert the number to the smaller type, effectively destroying the number. Thus it's important that you not mix types unless absolutely necessary and that you be aware of the values those types can hold.

You can also explicitly force C to make any of these conversions using *type casting*. When placed in front of any value, a type name in parentheses will convert the value to that type. For example, the following statement converts the number 56 to a character:

a = (char) 56;

C will automatically use such type casts in the program wherever it thinks necessary. For example, Figure 4-3 would be interpreted by C as the code shown in Figure 4-4.

Figure 4-4. Automatic Type Casting

```
int a;
a = 5;
a = (int) 4.5;
a = (int) 'f';
```

In most cases, it isn't necessary to use such casts. As you'll see later on in this book, type casting is necessary in certain cases where C is more type-sensitive or where C becomes confused as to the type being used.

These basic types are extended in C by larger and smaller versions of the basic types. These new versions allow you to reduce the amount of storage used by variables and to increase the range of values that a variable can hold. There are actually three types of integers in C as shown in Figure 4-5.

Figure 4-5. Three Types of Integer Variables

Name	Size	Range
char	One byte	−128 to 127
short int	Two bytes	−32768 to 32767
int	Two bytes	−32768 to 32767
long int	Four bytes	−2,147,483,648 to 2,147,483,647

In *Turbo C,* short ints are almost never used because they are identical to normal ints. Keep in mind that this might not be the case in other implementations of C. For example, under UNIX C, ints are four bytes while short ints are only two bytes.

Floats come in three types as shown in Figure 4-6.

Figure 4-6.

Name	Size	Range
float	Four bytes	3.4E−38 to 1.7E38
double	Eight bytes	1.7E−308 to 1.7E308
long double	Eight bytes	1.7E−308 to 1.7E308 (in version 1.5)
long double	Ten bytes	3.4E−4932 to 1.2E4932 (in versions after 1.5)

Long doubles are included only for compatibility with other versions of C.

Integers are much more accurate than floats. Because floats (and doubles) are able to hold such a large range of numbers, they cannot be perfectly accurate. They're accurate enough for most purposes, but bear in mind that any float might be inaccurate by 0.00001 percent, and any double, by 0.0000000001 percent.

You may also specify whether or not any variable can take on negative values. Normally half of a variable's range is negative. If the type is prefixed by the *unsigned* keyword, then that value may only take on positive values. Thus, while a char ranges from −128 to 127, an unsigned char ranges from 0 to 255.

Note that these modifiers produce entirely new types. An unsigned short int is an entirely different type from a long int, and it should be treated as such.

Also note that the keyword *int* can be dropped from the assignment if either the *long* or *unsigned* keywords are used. Thus a long is equivalent to a long int and an unsigned long int is equivalent to an unsigned long. Figure 4-7 contains a complete list of types. Types listed on the same line are equivalent.

Figure 4-7. Equivalent Variable Types

char	signed char		
unsigned char			
int	signed int	short int	short signed int
unsigned int	unsigned	unsigned short int	unsigned short
long	long int	signed long int	signed long
unsigned long	unsigned long int		
float			
double			
long double			

There are only eight variations of the basic types, but they may be written in 20 different ways. It's good practice to use the leftmost versions of each type name. Since most programmers use these names, they've become somewhat standardized, but keep in mind that programs could contain any of the 20 type names.

This is only the beginning. There is a whole set of other types and pointers to go with them. The types shown above are only the basic types used for most simple programming tasks. The rest will be described in later chapters.

Chapter 5

Simple Math

You must be able to assign more than just single values to a variable. When a statement is executed, C places the value of a variable on the right side of the expression in the variable on the left. See the code in Figure 5-1.

Figure 5-1. Assigning a Value to a Variable Through Resolution of an Expression

```
int a,b,c;

a = 5;
b = a;
c = b;
```

In addition, any mathematical operations on the right side of the equals sign are performed. When the statement a = b + c is executed in Figure 5-2, the variables *b* and *c* would be replaced with the numbers 5 and 4. These would then be added, and the number 9 would be placed in *a*.

Figure 5-2. Evaluating an Expression and Placing the Value in a Variable

```
int a,b,c;

b = 5;
c = 4;
a = b + c;
```

Four basic operations are available:

+   Addition
−   Subtraction
*   Multiplication
/   Division

All operations in C operate on values of type double to produce maximum accuracy. C converts all values to doubles before the operation and converts the result to the appropriate type after it has been evaluated.

C also provides the modulus operator. Its symbol is the percent sign (%). The modulus operator takes two numbers and returns the remainder left when the second number is divided into the first. Thus, 8 % 3 = 2. Unlike the four basic operators, % only returns integers.

Precedence

Every operation in C has a property called *precedence*, which is used to determine the order of mathematical operations. Often the computer will run into expressions that have two possible interpretations as in Figure 5-3. The operation with the highest precedence is always performed first. If the precedences are equal, the leftmost expression is performed first.

Figure 5-3. Precedence of Leftmost Operation Among Operations of Equivalent Precedence

a + b − c	a / b * c
is	is
(a + b) − c	(a / b) * c
not	not
a + (b − c)	a / (b * c)

Parentheses can be used to modify the order in which mathematical expressions are performed. The entire expression inside a set of parentheses will be evaluated before it's applied to any operations outside of the parentheses. Therefore, 1 / (2 + 3) is $\frac{1}{5}$. Without the parentheses, the expression would resolve as if it were (1 / 2) + 3, or 3½.

In C, the equal sign is considered an operator just like any other. It has a precedence lower than any of the operations that you've seen so far. Thus an assignment is always performed last. This will become important later on when you learn about conditional operators.

The designers of C were typical programmers. They hated to type. You'll find there are a number of features of C designed specifically to cut down on unnecessary typing.

Most programs will contain some expression of the form a = a + 10. You'll want to take a value out of a variable, do something to it, and return it to the same variable. C provides a whole set of operators to do just this. All come in the form ‹OP› = where ‹OP› is the operation you wish performed. For example, a + = 10 is equivalent to a = a + 10. These operators all have the same precedence as the assignment operator. Figure 5-4 contains some examples.

Figure 5-4. Examples of Shortcuts Using the Assignment Operator

Expression	Shortcut
a = a + 10	a + = 10
b = b * 8	b * = 8
pay = pay − (rate + hours * 10)	pay − = rate + hours * 10

Two additional operators allow you to increment and decrement a variable. The operator + + adds 1 to a variable, and − − subtracts 1 from it. These operators may either precede or follow the variable on which they operate. If the operator precedes the variable, then the operator will change its contents before it's used in the expression. If the operator follows, the contents will be changed afterward. Note that these operators are the only way to modify a variable without the assignment operator. Figure 5-5 contains some examples of these operators.

Figure 5-5. Increment and Decrement Operators

Expression	Shortcut
a = a + 1;	a + +;
b = a; a = a + 1;	b = a + +
a = a − 1; b = a;	b = − − a;
a + +; a = a + 1; b = a;	a + = 2; b = a;

These operators can be a little confusing at first. They can also be dangerous. Certain expressions, especially those in which the incremented variable appears twice, can have

ambiguous meanings—for instance, a = (5 * a++) + a or a
+ = a++. You're never required to use these shortcuts.
They're provided for your convenience. Figure 5-6 contains
an example of a somewhat confusing C construction.

Figure 5-6. A Confusing C Construction

```
#include <stdio.h>

main()
{
   int a=5;

   a *= a++;
   printf("a is %d\n",a);
   a = 5;
   a *= ++a;
   printf("a is %d\n",a);
}
```

The printed value of variable *a* will first be 26 and then
36. Why? A simple way to understand such an expression is
to move the autoincrement either before or after the expression, depending on whether it appears before or after the
variable. This is done in Figure 5-7.

Figure 5-7. Simplified Version of Program in Figure 5-6

```
#include <stdio.h>

main()
{
   int a=5;

   a *= a;
   a++;
   printf("a is %d\n",a);
   a = 5;
   a++;
   a *= a;
   printf("a is %d\n",a);
}
```

Compare the two programs. Figure 5-7 should make clear exactly what is happening and why you get the results you see.

A final problem with the autoincrement and autodecrement operators occurs in expressions like a + + +b. What does this mean? All operators have a certain right or left *associativity*. Associativity determines to which variable the operator is bound most tightly. The + + and − − operators are left-associative, thus in the expression a + + +b, the + + operator is more tightly bound to a variable on the left *(a)* and the expression will be evaluated as a + + +b.

As you can see, the autoincrement and autodecrement operators do have some intricacies of which you must be aware. However, you'll often find them very useful.

There are some additional operators in C, but these deal with more complicated features, and they'll be described later. Many mathematical functions, such as square roots and tangents, don't have operators. Instead, special *functions* are used to evaluate these expressions. These also will be described in later chapters.

Chapter 6
Conditional Operations

A *conditional statement* is a statement that causes an operation to take place only when certain conditions are met. Conditional statements are often called *if statements*. Before you can learn about if statements, you need to learn how C treats TRUE/FALSE values. In many languages, Boolean values are treated specially. A Boolean value may not be mixed with other types. This isn't the case in C. C has no Boolean type. Instead, integers are used to store TRUE/FALSE values. The number 0 is used to represent FALSE. Any other number represents TRUE.

It's often a good idea to add the following definitions to a program to help remind yourself of this fact. The use of the define statement will be described more fully in the next chapter. The following lines associate a name with a number:

#define TRUE 1
#define FALSE 0

With these definitions, you can use the words TRUE and FALSE instead of the numbers 1 and 0 to represent TRUE and FALSE. The #define compiler directive will be described more fully in the next chapter.

An if statement is used to execute a block of code only if a certain condition is true. The syntax is fairly simple: The word *if* is followed by an expression in parentheses and a block. If the expression is true, the block is executed. Figure 6-1 contains an example of a simple if statement.

Figure 6-1. If Statement

```
if (1)
  printf("The statement is true.\n");
```

You can put any expression in the parentheses. You can use any of the expressions discussed in the previous chapters, but they don't make much sense in a conditional.

In most if statements, you'll use one of the relational or equality operators. These are operators just like mathematical operators. They take two numbers and return either TRUE or FALSE depending on whether or not the expression is true. These operators are listed in Figure 6-2.

Figure 6-2. Equality and Relational Operators

Example	Meaning	Explanation
a = = b	Equality	TRUE if a and b are equal
a != b	Inequality	TRUE if a and b are not equal
a < b	Less than	TRUE if a is less than b
a > b	Greater than	TRUE if a is greater than b
a < = b	Less than or equal	TRUE if a less than or equal to b
a > = b	Greater than or equal	TRUE if a is greater than or equal to b

Boolean operators always have lower precedence than any of the equality or relational operators as well as the assignment operator. Thus all operations on either side of the expression are evaluated before the expression itself is evaluated. Consider the if statement in Figure 6-3.

Figure 6-3. An If Statement Using a Relational Operator

```
main()
{
   int a,b;

   a = 2;
   b = 4;
   if(a*4 <= b+4)
     printf("Will this print?\n");
}
```

When the if statement is executed, the expression in parentheses must be evaluated. Taking the operators in order of precedence, this expression is reduced in the following five steps:

a * 4 < = b + 4
2 * 4 < = b + 4
8 < = b + 4
8 < = 4 + 4
8 < = 8
1

Because 1 is considered to be TRUE, the expression is TRUE and the block — a single printf( ) in this case — is executed.

As mentioned before, the assignment is an operator like any other. All operators return some value and assignment is no exception. This return value is usually ignored as the programmer is more concerned with the effect on the variable than the return value. This return value can be useful. The assignment operator always returns the value assigned. Consider the if statement in Figure 6-4.

Figure 6-4. Using the Return Value

```
a = 23;
b = -4;
if (c = a + b - 4 != a - 4 + b)
    printf("Nope, not equal\n");
```

Taken step by step, the expression is reduced like this:

c = a + b − 4 != a − 4 + b
c = 23 + b − 4 != a − 4 + b
c = 23 + − 4 − 4 != a − 4 + b
c = 19 − 4 != a − 4 + b
c = 15 != a − 4 + b
c = 15 != 23 − 4 + b
c = 15 != 19 + b
c = 15 != 19 + −4
c = 15 != 15
c = 0
0

The expression is FALSE, so the printf( ) never gets executed.

The if statement causes program flow to branch off in one direction if a certain condition is met or to fall through if it isn't. There's a simple modification of the if statement that will cause program flow to split into two directions — one if the expression is TRUE and another if it's FALSE. This modification is the *else statement*.

Any legal if statement may be followed immediately by the word *else* and a statement (or a block containing multiple statements). The statements in this block will be executed only if the expression in the preceding if statement is FALSE. Figure 6-5 contains an example of a simple if-else statement.

Figure 6-5. Using an If-Else Statement

```
main()
{
  int a=4;

  if (a == 3)
    printf("a is 3!\n");
  else
    printf("a is not 3!\n");
}
```

The else statement must always directly follow an if statement. As with the if statement, the statement controlled by the else statement may be a single statement or it may be a number of statements inside a block.

Note to Pascal programmers: The statement preceding the else command ends with a semicolon. This is one of a few annoying little differences between Pascal and C that can trip you up. Unlike Pascal, C requires that every statement end with a semicolon, even if it's at the end of the block. The sole exception to this is a function declaration, which will be described later.

Chapter 7

Compiler Directives

A compiler directive is a command used by the compiler to determine how to compile a program. Once the program is compiled, all compiler directives are discarded. In theory, none of these compiler directives are actually a part of C. In practice, they're so important that they might as well be. This chapter will describe some of the most common compiler directives.

The #include Directive

The #include directive allows you to include text from other files into the file containing the directive. The #include directive must be followed by a filename enclosed either in angle brackets (< >) or double quotation marks (" ").

If the filename is enclosed in double quotation marks, *Turbo C* will look in the current working directory for that file and will load all text in the file into the program at the point where the directive is located. This is useful if you have a group of statements that are used in a number of different files. They could be placed in their own file which could be #included in each of the other programs.

If the filename is enclosed in angle brackets, *Turbo C* will look in the include files directory for the file to include. This directory is intended mainly for *Turbo C* header files. For example, the file STDIO.H must be included if you're to use any of the C input/output functions. You'll see the line #include ‹stdio.h› at the beginning of nearly every C program.

The #define Directive

The #define directive is used to increase program readability. The #define is a directive to the C macro preprocessor. This preprocessor examines a file before it's compiled, inserting included files as directed, replacing defined strings with their values, and expanding macro calls to their given definitions. For example, if a line containing

define NUM_APP number_of_appointments

appeared in a file, all occurrences of NUM_APP would be replaced with number_of_appointments. This allows you to give commonly used constants, such as 4048, more meaningful names, such as SCREEN_SIZE. Later on, you'll see how #define can be used to create powerful macro calls.

It's common practice to put all #defines at the top of the program. This is by no means a requirement. It's also traditional to make all such definitions completely uppercase. This isn't a requirement, either, but only a convention.

The #ifdef Directive

Another important compiler directive is the #ifdef directive. All statements between the #ifdef directive and the next #endif directive will be compiled only if the word following the #ifdef statement has been defined previously.

A word may have been defined in one of two ways. It may be defined with the #define directive as described above, or it may be defined by the compiler. To define a word in the interactive environment, enter the options menu; choose the compiler option and then the defines option. This will open up a one-line box. Enter the word here (multiple words should be separated by semicolons). These words then will be defined in any program.

To define a word in the command line version of *Turbo C,* use the -d option. The word following the -d option will be defined in the program to be compiled.

What is the use of all this? Here's an example. Suppose you wanted to write two versions of a program. One version is a nifty program. The other is a nifty program with some networking features added. Do these two programs need to occupy separate files? Not at all. Consider Figure 7-1.

Figure 7-1. Using Conditional Branching at Compile Time

```
#include <stdio.h>

nifty statement;
nifty statement;
nifty statement;
#ifdef NETWORK
networking statement;
#endif
nifty statement;
nifty statement;
```

The compiled networking version contains all the nifty statements as well as the networking statement. The compiled normal version contains just the nifty statements but not the networking statement. Both programs are compiled from the same source file. To compile the networking version, you'd use TCC -dNETWORK NIFTY.C from the command line, or you'd add NETWORK to the definition list in the interactive environment. To compile the standard version, you'd use TCC NIFTY.C from the command line, or the interactive equivalent.

One variation on #ifdef which you may run into is the defined( ) function. This is used in conjunction with the standard #if directive to produce an #if defined( ).

#if defined(NETWORK)

is identical to

#ifdef NETWORK

The function defined(NETWORK) is TRUE if NETWORK is defined and is FALSE if it isn't defined. This function could be used in an expression (though it's hard to imagine a case when you'd need to).

Another common use is with include files. Often an included file will itself include other files. This can be a problem. Suppose you have a file called NETWORK.H that includes MYSTUFF.H. You also have a file called MAIN.H that includes MYSTUFF.H and NETWORK.H. This will cause the compiler to attempt to include the contents of MYSTUFF.H twice. How do you prevent this?

The directive #ifndef will help. This command is the opposite of the #ifdef command. It will cause compilation of the statements it controls only if the word isn't defined. Suppose mystuff.h contained the text shown in Figure 7-2.

Figure 7-2. mystuff.h

```
#ifndef MYSTUFF
#define MYSTUFF
contents of mystuff.h
#endif
```

The first time the compiler includes this file, the word *MYSTUFF* is undefined, so the rest of the file will be compiled. MYSTUFF is defined in the file. If the compiler attempts to include the file a second time, the #ifndef MYSTUFF directive will find MYSTUFF defined and won't compile the contents of the file.

The #if Directive

The #if directive is even more flexible. If the value following it is 0, the statements between it and the #endif aren't compiled; otherwise, they are. The value following this directive can be a number or a previously defined word. Note that the word must have been given a value. In the example in Fig-

ure 7-1, #if NETWORK wouldn't have worked since NET-
WORK wasn't given a value; it simply was defined. To use
#if instead of #ifdef, you'd need to use TCC -
dNETWORK=1 rather than TCC -dNETWORK. The latter
never gives a value to NETWORK.

The keyword #else can be used with any of the #if commands. This command must be placed between an #if statement and its matching #endif statement. When this is done,
all commands before the #else command are compiled only
if the #if condition was met. All commands after the #else
statement are compiled only if the #if condition isn't met.
This allows you to performs actions as shown in Figure 7-3.

Figure 7-3. Using #else

```
nifty statement;
#ifdef NET
nifty networking statement;
#else
nifty non-networking statement;
#endif
nifty statement;
```

In addition, the command #else if combines an #else directive and an #if directive. The controlled statements are
compiled only if the else path is taken.

Once something has been defined, you cannot change
its definition. You can, however, remove a definition (allowing it to be defined again with a new value). This is done
with the #undef directive. This must be followed with a previously defined word. The definition then will be removed.
Consider Figure 7-4.

Figure 7-4. Using #undef

```
int answer;
#define answer 42
a = a + answer;
#undef answer
answer = a;
```

When is answer a variable and when is it a constant
with a value of 42? Remember that macros are replaced with
their definitions before compilation. The compiler would see
Figure 7-4 as Figure 7-5.

Figure 7-5. Compiler's View of Program in Figure 7-4

```
int answer;
a = a + 42;
answer = a;
```

You may find it useful to see how the preprocessor uses
these compiler directives. *Turbo C* includes a special program
that will create a new file using all compiler directives. This
program is called CPP. CPP takes all the same commands as
does TCC. Instead of producing an .EXE file, it produces a .I
file containing your program after all compiler directives
have been followed. This file cannot be compiled.

Be forewarned: the standard .H files are quite large. You
will find that even a very small file will expand greatly after
a few of these header files are added.

CPP isn't often used, but it's very handy, especially for
the novice C programmer. The best way to learn about compiler directives is to use CPP to see exactly what they're doing.

These compiler directives aren't part of the C language
itself, but they are used in every standard C compiler and
are considered to be a part of standard C. Because they're a
product of the UNIX operating system, you'll find that
they're used with many different compilers. The UNIX Pascal
compiler is a good example.

Chapter 8

Loops

C provides three different types of loops. Programmers will instantly recognize *for loops*. As you will see, for loops in C are very flexible. In addition, two different types of *while loops* are also available.

Most languages have some kind of for loop. In theory, a for loop repeats a statement a certain number of times. For loops in C are more flexible than this, however. There are a number of different ways that C can determine the number of times to execute the statements in the loop. The syntax of a for loop is

for (Initial condition; Final condition; repeated statements)
  block;

The compiler will place the statements in the initial condition section before the block. It will place the repeated statements before the end of the block. During execution, the final condition will be tested each time the end of the block is reached. If the condition is true, the entire block will be repeated. Otherwise the program will exit the loop.

For example, consider the loop in Figure 8-1.

Figure 8-1. A For Loop

```
#include <stdio.h>

main()
{
int i;

for(i = 0; i < 23; i++)
  {
    printf("The start of the loop\n");
    printf("i is %d\n",i);
  }
    printf("The end of the loop\n");

}
```

The compiler will interpret this as shown in Figure 8-2.

Figure 8-2. The Compiler's Interpretation of the Example in Figure 8-1

```
int i;

i=0;
{
  printf("The start of the loop\n");
  printf("i is %d\n",i);
  printf("The end of the loop\n");

  i++;
}
if ( i<23 ) repeat; /* Not legal C */
```

As you can see,

for(i = 0; i < 23; i + +)

means *repeat the block with* i *taking values from 0 to 22, adding 1 to* i *each time.*

In most cases, you can use the above example as a template for loops. The first number determines that value at which *i* begins. To find out the number of times the loop will be executed, subtract the first number from the second. Thus, to repeat a statement ten times, you'd use the command

for (i = 0; i < 10; i + +)

The loop control variable, *i* in the previous example, can be any declared character or integer variable. It has been traditional among programmers to use the variables *i, j, k, l,* and so on, as loop control variables, with *i* controlling the outermost loop, *j* the next one in, and so on. This practice is a holdover from the days of Fortran. In Fortran, these variables are declared as integers automatically, while all other variables are declared as floats.

While this is a common practice, it isn't always good programming style. If you're counting a specific thing, it's usually better to name the variable after that thing. For example, the loop

for (day_of_week = SUNDAY; day_of_week< = SATURDAY; day_of_week+ +)

is easier to understand than

for (i = 0; i<7; i+ +)

For loops are much more flexible than this, however. The starting condition and repeated statements sections can contain more than one statement. The statements in each section are separated by commas (*not* semicolons, as you might expect). This allows you to do things with for loops that you might not think possible at first. Consider Figure 8-3.

Figure 8-3. A Loop Awaiting Input

```
#include <stdio.h>

main()
{
  int total, input=-1;

  for ( total=0; input!=0; total+=input )
  {
    printf("Enter a number: ");
    scanf("%d",&input);
  }
 printf("The total is %d\n",total);
}
```

In Figure 8-3, the initial and end conditions are apparently unrelated. Unlike the previous loop, this for loop doesn't repeat a set number of times. It will repeat the block until the variable input equals 0. This variable is dependent on user input. The initial condition is used only to clear a variable that isn't directly related to the ending condition.

The repeated statement also isn't directly connected to the test condition.

You also could use a for loop to repeat until a certain key is pressed as in Figure 8-4.

Figure 8-4. Loop Awaiting a Certain Keypress

```
#include <stdio.h>

main()
{
for(printf("Starting loop\n");getch()!='q';printf("Hit 'q' to quit\n"))
printf("Looped statements\n");
}
```

While loops are simply a generalized version of for loops. Only the test condition is present. There are no initial conditions or repeated statements. Figure 8-5 contains an example of a while loop.

Figure 8-5. A While Loop

```
#include <stdio.h>

main()
{
printf("Starting loop\n");

while(getch()!='q')

    {
     printf("Looped statements\n");
     printf("Hit 'q' to quit\n");
    }
}
```

This code will have the same effect as the code in Figure 8-4. Obviously a while loop can do everything that a for loop can do. The advantage of the for loop is that it pulls the important parts of the loop into one statement. This allows for greater readability and program debugging. There are times when the structure of the for loop won't be as readable as the one in Figure 8-4. Usually, for loops should be restricted to loops whose flow is fairly simple. If a loop will have a number of different ending conditions, you should write a while loop.

While loops always test the condition before the main body of the loop is executed. Often you'll want to test this condition at the end of the loop. This can be done with the *do loop*. A do loop is similar to a while loop, except that in a while loop, the while statement appears at the end of the block, and in the do loop, the word *do* appears at the beginning.

Figure 8-6 contains a typical do loop.

Figure 8-6. A Do Loop

```
#include <stdio.h>

main()
{
    do

    {
     printf("Looped statements\n");
     printf("Hit 'q' to quit\n");
    }
     while(getch()!='q');
}
```

This will produce results that are nearly identical to Figures 8-4 and 8-5.

The major difference is that while loops check the condition at the beginning of the loop, but do loops check the condition at the end. The net effect is that the code inside a do loop is always executed at least once, but the code inside a while loop may not be executed at all, if the condition fails immediately.

Chapter 9

Input/Output

This chapter will describe some of the standard *Turbo C* input/output functions. In C, there are no input or output statements. Instead, you use *standard functions*. A function is a section of code that has its own name. There are a number of tasks which, while commonly needed by the programmer, aren't available in the language itself. C includes these tasks as standard functions. These tasks include printing to the screen, reading from the keyboard and other, similar tasks.

To use a function, give its name followed by parentheses containing a list of parameters. Parameters are variables that are sent to the code in the function.

Before you can use any of the standard functions, you must include the appropriate header file. A header file contains special information about functions. There are a number of different header files containing declarations of a number of different functions.

The function putch( ) will send a single character to the screen. It's located in the *library* stdio. (A library is simply a set of functions.) To use any function in this library, you must have the line

#include <stdio.h>

at the beginning of the file.

Putchar( ) is a fairly simple function. It takes a single character as a parameter and prints it to the screen. The character may be sent to the function alone or may be sent in a variable. Figure 9-1 contains an example of the use of this function.

Figure 9-1. Calling a Standard Function

```
#include <stdio.h>
main()
{
  char a = 'e';
  int i;

  for ( i=0; i<5; i++)
  {
    putchar('h');
    putchar(a);
    putchar(a);
  }
}
```

Output:

heeheeheeheehee

Some functions return values to the main program. The returned value can be assigned to a variable. The function getch( ), also in stdio, reads a single key from the keyboard and returns it to the calling routine. It has no parameters. Figure 9-2 contains an example of its use.

Figure 9-2. Using getch( )

```
#include <stdio.h>

main()
{
  char ch;

  do
  {
    ch = getch();
    putchar( ch );
  }
  while ( ch != 'q' );
}
```

The program in Figure 9-2 will echo all keystrokes until the letter *q* is pressed. Each keystroke is read by the function getch( ) and is placed in *ch*. The function putchar( ) then takes the character in *ch* and prints it to the screen.

Function calls can be used as parameters to other functions. For example, in the preceding example, the lines

ch = getch( );
putchar(ch);

could be replaced with the single statement

putchar(getch( ));

In this case, getch( ) reads a keystroke and sends it directly to putchar( ).

But wait. If you do that, your loop won't work correctly. The variable *ch* will no longer contain the character just read. This can be solved easily. Recall that the assignment operator returns the value just assigned. The new routine should actually look like Figure 9-3.

Figure 9-3. Altered Version of Program in Figure 9-2

```
#include <stdio.h>
main()
{
   char ch;

   do
   {
     putchar( ch = getch() );
   }
   while( ch != 'q' );
}
```

The putchar( ) function actually returns a value. (As you may have guessed, you don't need to use the value returned by a function.) The putchar( ) function returns the character printed. Most of the time, you'll want to ignore this, but in the next example, it will greatly shorten your program. Why not place the call to putchar( ) in the loop itself? (See Figure 9-4.) This may seem a little strange at first. Think of it this way: *Get a character and print it to the screen. If the character just printed is not a q, repeat the loop.*

Figure 9-4. An Even Shorter Version

```
#include <stdio.h>

main()
{


    {
       while(putchar(getch()) != 'q');
    }


}
```

Printing any large amount of text one character at a time would get very tedious.

Most output is performed with the function printf( ). This function is far more complicated than putchar( ) and can handle all types of formatted output.

The printf( ) function can take a variable number of parameters. The first parameter is the format specification. The printf( ) statement then may contain one or more values. These values will be printed according to the format in the format specification.

The format specification is sent to printf( ) in a string. If there are no formatting commands in the string, printf( ) will print the string as it is. A string is any list of characters surrounded by double quotation marks (" ").

printf("This is a string!");

In this example the format specification contains *This is a string!* Because there are no formatting commands, this string will be printed as it is, sending *This is a string!* to the screen.

Formatting commands allow you to take a value and place it into the middle of a format specification. In this manner, the contents of variables may be sent to the screen. All formatting commands begin with a percent sign (%) and one or more letters. This command will mark the place in the string where the value is to be inserted. The simplest formatting commands consist of a single character.

Following is a list of simple formatting commands:

Formatting Command	Meaning
%d	Integer
%i	Integer
%o	Octal integer
%u	Unsigned integer
%x	Hexadecimal integers (small letters)
%f	Floating point, no exponent
%e	Floating point, with exponent
%g	Floating point, possible exponent
%c	Single character
%s	String

Each value in the parameter list of printf( ) will be matched with a formatting command in the format specification. The first value will match the first format command, the second value will match the second format command, and so on. C doesn't check to make sure that the types match. It will attempt to change the variable to the appropriate type (thus you can print character values as integers or integers as floating-point numbers if you so desire). See Figure 9-5.

Figure 9-5. Printing Integers

```
#include <stdio.h>

main()
{
     int a,b;
     a = 5;
     b = 6;


     printf("a is %d, b is %d",a,b);

}
```

When this runs, it will produce the following output:

a is 5, b is 6

The first format specification is replaced by the value in *a*; the second, by the value in *b*.

Normally values will take only the space necessary to contain them. It's possible to specify the width each value is to take by placing the number of characters between the percent sign and the format character. See Figure 9-6.

Figure 9-6. Formatting Output

```
#include <stdio.h>

main()
{
     int a,b;
     a = 5;
     b = 6;


     printf("a contains %5d, b contains %5d",a,b);

}
```

When run, this produces the following output:

a contains   5, b contains   6

Now both values occupy five spaces regardless of how many spaces are required by the output.

The width may be larger than one digit. If it begins with a zero, zeros will be used to mark unused portions of the field. See Figure 9-7.

Figure 9-7. Filled Formatting

```
#include <stdio.h>

main()
{

    int a,b;
    a = 5;
    b = 6;


        printf("a contains %05d, b contains %5d",a,b);


}
```

The following is the output:

a contains 00005, b contains   6

Notice that the first variable is printed using leading zeros and the second is printed with leading spaces.

You can also specify the number of decimal places used when a floating-point variable is printed. This is done by following the width specifier with a decimal point and a number of decimal places. For example, the command

%7.2f

would print a floating-point number with only two decimal places (seven characters overall). Consider Figure 9-8.

Figure 9-8. Formatting Floats

```
main()
{
    float a;
    int b;

    a = 5.678;
    b = 90;


    printf("The float is %05.2f, the int is %d",a,b);


}
```

The output will be

The float is 05.68, the int is 90

The printf( ) function has a keyboard-reading counterpart called scanf( ). The scanf( ) function has the same parameters as printf( ). Instead of printing the format specification, scanf( ) reads it from the keyboard.

A simple example of scanf( ) would be the statement

scanf("A test");

This wouldn't be a very good example, as this commands says *read the characters "A test"* from the keyboard (obviously not a very useful thing to do). If the characters read from the keyboard don't match the characters in the format specification, an error is produced.

Usually scanf( ) will contain only formatting commands. These commands are identical to those used in printf( ). Each command is used to read the appropriate value from the keyboard. Each value is placed in a variable in the parameter list of scanf( ). For example, to read an integer into a variable called *a*, you'd use

scanf("%d",&a);

Why the ampersand (&)? The scanf( ) function requires the address of the variable. The ampersand supplies this address (more on this in later chapters). Consider Figure 9-9.

Figure 9·9. Using scanf( )

```
#include <stdio.h>

main()
{

    int num;


    printf("Enter a number:");
    scanf("%d",&num);
    printf("\nThe number is %d!",num);



}
```

The scanf( ) statement will read a single number and place it in the variable *num*.

The \n in the printf( ) statement is one of a series of control commands. These commands send special characters to the screen. The command \n sends a *newline* character (which breaks the current line and begins printing at the left margin of the next line) to the screen, starting a new line. Other control commands are shown below.

Command	Action
\a	Bell
\b	Backspace
\f	Clearscreen (Formfeed)
\n	Newline
\r	Carriage return
\t	Horizontal tab (usually eight spaces)
\v	Vertical tab
\###	Character with octal ASCII value ###
\x###	Character with hex ASCII value ###

Any other character following a backslash (\) will be placed in the string as it is. This includes characters that cannot normally be placed inside of strings, such as single or double quotation marks (' ' or " "), and backslashes. These control commands may be placed in any string. They aren't tied directly to scanf( ) and printf( ).

There are a number of other functions included with *Turbo C* that perform I/O and other important tasks. The calling conventions for these functions are similar to those of the functions described here. The *Turbo C* reference manuals describe these functions in more detail than is possible in this book.

Chapter 10

Switches, Breaks, and Labels

An if statement is the only branching statement necessary for most circumstances. There are times, however, when you'll need a more powerful branching statement.

The Switch Block

The switch statement allows you to choose between a whole set of different possibilities. A switch block is a fairly complex set of code. There are four keywords that usually are used with switch statements:

Switch statement	Specifies the expression that selects which option will be executed
Case keyword	Marks the beginning of an option
Break keyword	Marks the end of an option
Default keyword	Marks an option that will be executed if no other option is selected

Figure 10-1 contains an example of a switch block showing some of the subtleties of this command.

Figure 10-1. The Components of a Switch Block in Context

```
#include <stdio.h>

main()
{
    int a;

    while((a = getch()) != 'q')

        switch(a)

    {
        case 'a': printf("Certainly a good choice!\n");
        break;

        case 'b': printf("This isn't bad, but...\n");
```

```
case 'c': printf("This is better.\n");
break;
case 'q': printf("This will never print...Why?\n");
break;
case 'x':

case 'y':

case 'z': printf("These are cool letters.\n");
break;

default: printf("Gee, I didn't think of that.\n");
break;

    }


}
```

You may wonder why the case for *q* will never be selected. Remember that this loop is dependent on your input. Once you enter a *q*, the program exits the loop, so the switch(a) never gets evaluated for a value of *q*.

The switch statement, like the if statement, takes a single expression. Unlike the if statement, the expression should return a valid integer type (char, int, or long). The statement then compares the result of this expression with each case in turn. When a match is found, program control is passed directly to the statement following the colon. Program flow then continues normally until a break statement is found, at which point control leaves the switch block. If no condition is met, control is passed to the statements following the default keyword.

Note that you can glue two case statements together by leaving off the break statement; this is known as allowing flow to *fall through*. If you press the C key at the top of the loop, only the words *this is better* will be printed. If, however, you press the B key, the words *This isn't bad, but* . . . . . will be printed; then, because no break is found, control will skip to the next case, find the next printf( ), and print *this is better*.

The break Statement

Switch statements in C are more free form than similar statements in other languages. They're actually built upon a number of other features of C. The break statement, for example, isn't restricted to a switch block. This statement causes control to leave the innermost for, while, or switch block. It could have been used in a loop as in Figure 10-2.

Figure 10-2. Using the break Statement

```
#include <stdio.h>

main()
{

    int i,ch;

    for(i=0;i<50;i++)
      {
        ch = getch();
        printf("%c",ch);
        if(ch == 'q')
            break;
      }
}
```

Normally this loop would read 50 characters, but because of the break statement, it might end prematurely.

It usually isn't a good idea to use break unless absolutely necessary (as in a switch statement). It can make programs very difficult to debug. Looking at the loop in Figure 10-2, it seems as if the loop can only end when *i* reaches 50. This isn't the case, however, as the break statement can also terminate the loop.

The continue Statement

A variation on break is continue. Like break, continue immediately jumps to the end of a loop. Unlike break, continue then continues execution of the loop. Figure 10-3 contains an example of this.

Figure 10-3. The continue Statement in Context

```
#include <stdio.h>

main()
{

    int i;

    for(i=0;i<20;i++)
      {
         if(i == 10)
              continue;
            printf("'i' is %d\n",i);



      }
 }
```

Because of the continue statement, the printf( ) won't be executed if *i* is 10. If the continue statement in Figure 10-3 were replaced by a break statement, the printf( ) would execute only for values of *i* less than 10. All execution of the loop would have been terminated, not just the current iteration, when *i* reached 10.

The goto Statement and Labels

The case statement is really only a variation on labels. A label provides a way of marking a piece of a program. You can then use another statement, goto, to pass control directly to this piece of code.

A label is any previously undeclared symbol followed by a colon. Any goto statement using this label will transfer control to this label. Figure 10-4 contains an example.

Figure 10-4. The goto Statement in Context

```
#include <stdio.h>

main()
{
        printf("This is the first statement.\n");
        goto a_label;
        printf("This statement will never be reached.\n");
a_label:
        printf("This statement will be reached.\n");

}
```

Because of the goto statement, the second printf( ) function call will never be executed. Control will pass directly from the goto statement to the statements following a _ label.

While goto statements may seem useful to you, use them with care. Programs with too many goto commands begin to resemble a bowl of spaghetti. Trying to determine where flow actually goes can become a nightmare. Most programmers avoid gotos wherever possible. Some languages don't even support them.

The most common use of goto statements in C is to jump to the end of the program. This is so common that it was made into a special function. The exit( ) function automatically exits the program. It takes one parameter, the exit status. This is used mainly by DOS. Typically, 0 denotes that the program terminated normally and any other number denotes an error (see Figure 10-5).

Figure 10-5. Using the exit( ) Function

```
#include <stdio.h>

main()
{
        int ch;

        printf("Whatever you do, do not hit 'x'\n");
        ch = getch();

        if(ch == 'x')
        {
                printf("Error!! I told you not to do that!\n");
                exit(1);

        }

}
```

Every program automatically does an exit(0) at the end of main( ), whether it's explicitly placed there or not.

The exit( ) function, like the many other statements and functions in this chapter, should be used with care. Heavy use of these statements and functions will decrease the readability of your program.

Chapter 11
Function Declarations

You have used some of the standard *Turbo C* functions. This chapter will show you how to create your own functions. These functions then can be used in your own programs and may appear in the same file as your main program, or they may reside in other files.

Why Break Code into Functions?

There are two reasons for breaking code into functions: clarity and program size.

Each function should contain a logically independent section of code. Before writing any code, break your program into sections. Each section should perform one action, such as adding to a database or drawing a single figure on the screen. If a piece of code cannot be described easily in a sentence or two, it should be broken into more than one function.

In addition, if you ever repeat a certain set of statements in more than one place in a program, these statements should be placed in a single function, and a call to the function should be used instead. This will help reduce the size of your program, thus increasing its efficiency.

The main( ) Function

All C programs are made up of a set of functions. At least one function, main( ), must always be present. The main( ) function is a very easy function to declare as there usually are no parameters. Other function declarations will be more complex, though not prohibitively so.

The Function Prototype

Every function declaration comes in two sections. The first section is the function prototype. This shows the compiler what arguments the function will take. This prototype should appear before the function is called. It's traditional to put these prototypes in special files called *header files* which are included at the beginning of any program that uses the corresponding functions. This is the purpose of the standard C header files such as STDIO.H. This file contains prototypes for such functions as printf( ) and scanf( ).

Once you've read this chapter, you may want to look at the header files to get a better idea of how they're written. Unless you're already familiar with pointers or files, much of it won't make sense, but these files do provide a good example of how to organize a header file.

Functions always have parameters and return values. Parameters are values sent by the calling program to the function. Return values are values sent by the function back to the main program. In order to compile a function call correctly, the compiler must know what these values will be.

A function prototype always consists of the function name followed by a pair of parentheses enclosing a set of parameter types which are separated by commas. The return type of the function is always placed in front of the function name. Like any statement, the prototype must end with a semicolon. The parameter type may include the parameter name, though this is optional. Figure 11-1 contains a few simple prototypes.

Figure 11-1. A Few Simple Prototypes

```
main()
{
   int add(int a,int b);
   int subtract(int a,int b);
   float multiply(float a,float b,int c,int d);
   void print_screen(void);
   void plot(int x,int y,char color);
   color(int x,int y);

}
```

The first two prototypes describe functions that take two integer parameters and return a single integer to the calling function. The third prototype describes a function that takes two floats and two integers and returns a single float. The next-to-the-last two functions show the use of a new type of variable. The *void* type is useful only in function declarations. This type actually means *no type*. It has no value, and it takes no space. It's useful mainly for saying *this function has no parameters*. In some cases, C assumes that a value with no specified type is an integer. Thus the compiler assumes that the last function

color(int x,int y)

returns an int. If you don't want a function to return anything, you should explicitly state this by declaring it to be type void.

While it's sometimes legal to leave off the int in a prototype, it's almost never a good idea. By explicitly stating type, you avoid becoming confused over what type actually is being used.

It's also a good idea to give parameters names in your prototypes. Though the compiler ignores these names, they can help make your header files easier to use as a reference list of your functions. Consider the fifth function in Figure 11-1. Which parameter specifies the color? Which parameter specifies the *x* coordinate? It's fairly easy to tell, isn't it? It would have been legal to have prototyped this function as

color(int,int);

Obviously this prototype would be less useful to the programmer.

Function Declaration

Once the function has been prototyped in the header file, it may be declared anywhere in the C file. Note that unlike some languages, C allows you to call a function before it's declared. The compiler needs only the prototype to compile a function call. A function declaration looks much like a prototype except that both parameter types and names are required and the ending semicolon is replaced with a block of code. Note that variable names used in the declaration need not match the names given in the prototype; however, the types *must match*. Figure 11-2 contains a declaration of the function add( ) that was prototyped in Figure 11-1.

Figure 11-2. Declaration of the Function add( )

```
int add(int a,int b)
{
  int c;
  c = a + b;
  return c;
}
```

The block controlled by the function may be any standard C block. It may contain any C statement or declaration (except other function declarations).

The return Statement

Another statement used in a functions is the return statement. The return statement immediately ends the function, sending a value back to the calling routine.

The type of the returned value must match the return type of the function. In most other respects this statement is similar to the break statement.

Figure 11-3 contains a listing of a program that includes this statement. Remember that you must create a header file containing the prototype for the add( ) function:

int add(int a,int b);

You'll see more about header files later.

Figure 11-3. Use of the return Statement

```
#include <stdio.h>
#include "add.h"

main()
{

    int a,b;

    a = 19;
    b = add(a,5);
    printf("%d",b);
    }

int add(int a,int b)

{
        int c;

        c = a + b;
        return c;


    }
```

Old and New Function Declarations

C has been changing over the years and there are a few
holdover features of which you should be aware. The above
declaration is a new style of declaration that has recently become the C standard. Previously, parameter types were listed after the parentheses but before the block. Parentheses
still contain a list of parameter names. The function in Figure
11-3 would be declared as in Figure 11-4.

Figure 11-4. The Old Way of Declaring Functions

```
main()

{

   int add(a,b)
   int a,b;
   {
     int c;
     c = a + b;
     return c;
   }

}
```

Turbo C fully supports such declarations. The names in the declaration must match those in the parentheses. They need not be in the same order. While there's no particular reason you should avoid this type of declaration, there's no particular reason why you should use it, either. The newer way is just as clear and requires less typing.

Chapter 12

Arrays

The previous chapters have described only the simple data types. In C, complex data types can be created from the simple data types.

The Array Operator

The first complex data type is the array. An array is an ordered sequence of variables of identical type, stored under a single name. An array is declared by listing a type, a name, and a number enclosed in square brackets. The number inside the square brackets represents the number of elements to create. Figure 12-1 shows a list of some simple arrays.

Figure 12-1. A List of Simple Arrays

Array	Description
int a[10];	An array of ten integers
float b[2];	An array of two real numbers
char a[40],buffer[256];	Two arrays of characters: one with 40 characters, one with 256
int many[100],one;	An array of 100 integers and a single integer variable

Accessing Arrays

To access a member of the array, specify the array name followed by a number in square brackets. This time, the number in the square brackets refers to the element to access. In C, element numbers always begin at 0. Figure 12-2 contains some examples of array accesses.

Figure 12-2. Array Access

Access	Explanation
a = many[54];	Set *a* to the fifty-fifth element in array many
b[5] + +;	Add 1 to the sixth element in *b*
c = sqr(a + buffer[9]);	Use the tenth element of buffer in an expression
i = 6; x = list[i];	Set *x* equal to the seventh element (element number 6) of list
i = 7; pointers[i] = 4;	The value of 4 is assigned to pointers[7]
data[pointers[i]] = 12	Set the fifth element (element number 4) of data to equal 12

An array element may be treated in exactly the same manner as a simple variable of the same type. It may be used anywhere a simple variable could be used: in assignments, expressions, parameter lists, and even array accesses.

It's possible to assign array variables immediately as they're declared. This is done using the assignment operator and a list of values between braces, separated by commas. If there are more elements than values, the remaining elements will be initialized to 0. If there are more values than elements, then the extra values will be discarded.

Figure 12-3 contains examples of arrays being assigned and declared. If the array is of type char, it may be initialized with a string. In this case, one letter is placed in each array element.

Figure 12-3. Assigning and Declaring Arrays

```
int a[10] = {4,5,6,7,8,9,10,11,12,13};
char a[4] = {'a','b','c','d'};
char hi[20] = "Hi there!";
```

Multidimensional Arrays

It's even possible to create arrays of arrays. Such arrays are called *multidimensional arrays*. They're created in C simply by using a number enclosed in square brackets for each dimension. Figure 12-4 contains some examples.

Figure 12-4. Multidimensional Arrays

Example	Explanation
int a;	An integer
int a[10];	An array of ten integers
int a[10][9];	A 10 × 9 array of integers
int a[4][4][4];	A 4 × 4 × 4 array of integers

Multidimensional arrays are accessed just as you might think: Each array operator moves one level down the list. For example, if you declared an array as

int a[10][9];

then the expression

a[4]

would refer to the fourth array of nine integers.

You can initialize multidimensional arrays in the same manner as one-dimensional arrays. Each value in the list is placed in each corresponding element of the array. The first subarray is filled first, then the second, and so on.

To a limited extent, you can refer to an entire array using just the name. While you cannot directly assign the entire contents of an array to another, you can pass an entire array as a parameter. The program in Figure 12-5 gives an example of this.

Figure 12-5. Passing an Array as a Parameter

```
#include <stdio.h>

int add(int a[10]);

int add(int a[10])
{
  int i;
  int answer = 0;

  for ( i=0; i<10; i++ )
  answer += a[i];
  return answer;
}

main()
{
  int d[10];
  int i;

  for ( i=0; i<10; i++ )
    d[i] = i*i;

  printf("%d\n",add(d));
}
```

In the call to the function add( ), the entire array is passed under the name alone (d). If you try to pass an array element to the function add( ), a type mismatch will result.

Mismatched Parameters

C takes a very liberal attitude toward matching parameters. Simple variables are all obvious. Ints match ints, floats match floats, and chars match chars. The complex types can act a little strangely.

According to the compiler, any array will always match any other array with the same base type. The base type of an array is the type upon which it was built. If the base types of your arrays don't match, you'll receive a warning message, assuming that you've turned on warning messages. You should keep the warning messages turned on. This will help you catch errors that would otherwise be missed. Warning messages are turned on through the options menu.

Your program will compile despite its mismatched arrays, though in all probability it won't work correctly.

Transferring the Contents of One Array to Another

Unfortunately you can't assign arrays to each other. C provides a function to copy the contents of one array to another, however. The memcpy( ) function takes three parameters:

Destination address
Source address
Number of bytes

It then will transfer that number of bytes from the source to the destination. At this point, another standard function, sizeof( ), comes in very handy. When given a variable or type, sizeof( ) returns the length, in bytes, of that variable or type. The address of an array is always the same as its name. Therefore, to transfer memory from one array to another, you can simply use the array names with memcpy( ). Figure 12-6 has some examples.

Figure 12-6. Transferring Values with Array Names

```
main()
{

int array_one[10];
int array_two[10];
int a,b=5;

memcpy(&a,&b,sizeof(int));
/* The equivalent of an integer assignment */

memcpy(array_one,array_two,sizeof(array_one));
/* Copy the contents of array_two to array_one */

memcpy(array_one,array_two,sizeof(int)*5);
/*Copy the first five elements of array_two to
        array_one */
```

```
memcpy(array_one,array_two+5,sizeof(int)*5);
/*Copy the last five elements of array_one to
        the first five elements of array_two */
}
```

The first example shows how simple variables could be used with memcpy( ). The ampersand (&) specifies the address of the variable.

The second example copies the entire contents of one array to another using sizeof( ) to determine the array size.

The last two examples show how the element size can be used to copy a section of one array to another. Note that when you add a number to an array name, the result is automatically an array beginning at that element. Thus if you add 5 to the address of an array of ten elements, the result is the address of an array of five elements beginning with the sixth element in the original array.

Warning: The sizeof( ) function won't work with arrays declared as parameters. If you try to find the size of such a parameter, the result will always be either 2 or 4 (you'll see why in later chapters). To find the actual size of the array, you should multiply the number of elements in the array by the size of the base type. This will always be accurate.

In general, you should avoid using arrays as parameters. Such parameters won't always act the way you expect. The sizeof( ) problem mentioned above is a good example. This isn't a bug in *Turbo C;* rather, this is an idiosyncrasy of the C language. In the next chapter, you'll see a way to pass large amounts of data to a function without using arrays.

Chapter 13

Pointers

A pointer is a variable that holds a memory address. You've already dealt with pointers in a few different ways. When you pass the address of a variable to scanf( ) with the & operator, you're passing a pointer to the variable.

The scanf( ) function only takes pointers. In addition, all character strings (delimited by quotation marks) are actually pointers to areas in memory. Finally, all array names actually are pointers to blocks of memory.

The Character String

The most frequently used pointer involves character strings. You've already seen a quotation mark delimited string constant. Such a string is created with quotation marks. The quotation marks cause all characters between them to be placed in memory at an address. This address is then returned to the program. If you place this value in a pointer variable, you can save and manipulate the string.

Pointer variables are created by the pointer operator. This operator is the asterisk (*). The pointer operator may be used with any type. This causes the variable to be a *pointer* to that type rather than causing the variable to *be* that type. A string is just a series of characters. The best way to reference this is as a pointer to a character (or, in this case, a pointer to characters).

Figure 13-1 contains an example of a character pointer in use.

Figure 13-1. A Character Pointer in Use

```
main()
{
  char *string;

  string = "this is the string";

  printf(string);
}
```

This declaration creates a pointer to a set of characters called string. At first, string is undefined, so the pointer doesn't actually point to anything. The assignment takes the address of the string and places it in this variable. This is then sent to printf( ).

Pointers and Arrays

Pointers have much in common with arrays. In fact, an array is just a special pointer called a *constant pointer*. It's constant in that, once set, it can never be changed. Therefore, any function that takes a character pointer will also take a character array.

Figure 13-1 could be rewritten as Figure 13-2.

Figure 13-2. Figure 13-1 Rewritten with a Character Array

```
main()
{
char string[20];

strcpy(string,"This is the string");

printf(string);
}
```

The strcpy( ) function is a cousin of memcpy( ). Unlike memcpy( ), it doesn't need to know the number of bytes to copy. All strings in C end with a special nonprinting character called *null* (ASCII value of 0). Strcpy( ) will copy all characters from the source to the destination until it encounters a null. It only works with strings.

As you can see, pointers can be used in a manner very similar to arrays. The major difference between the two is that a pointer doesn't automatically have memory space reserved for it.

The malloc( ) Function

In one sense, pointers might be thought of as variable-length arrays. In order to allocate space to a pointer, use malloc( ). This function reserves a portion of memory and returns a void pointer to that area of memory. A void pointer is a special pointer that matches any other pointer type. The malloc( ) function takes one parameter: the number of bytes to be used.

Figure 13-3 contains an example of how malloc( ) could be used to create an array of ten elements. Note that you must include ALLOC.H to use malloc( ).

Figure 13-3. The malloc( ) Function in Context

```
#include <alloc.h>
main()
{
   int *d;
   int i;

   d = malloc(10 * sizeof(int));
   for ( i=0; i<10; i++ )
     d[i] = i*i;

   printf("%d\n",d[5]);
}
```

The malloc( ) statement creates space for ten integers and assigns to *d* a pointer to that space. You can then use *d* just like an array.

Remember that an array is also just a pointer to an area of memory. Another difference between a standard array and a pointer array created with malloc( ) is that the size of an array created with malloc( ) doesn't need to be known when the program is written. The value given to malloc( ) could just as easily have been in a variable read from the keyboard.

Another advantage of pointer arrays is that you can return memory to the free memory pool when you're done with it. The free( ) function takes one parameter: a pointer that has been given space by malloc( ). All such space will be returned to the free memory pool. The pointer then should be set to null (a pointer pointing to nothing).

You should never try to free a pointer that doesn't have memory allocated to it. This will cause your program to crash. Always set your pointers to null if they have no space allocated to them.

Never free a pointer that is null. You can use

if (pointer != NULL) free(pointer);

or simply

if (pointer) free(pointer);

to make sure you never free a null pointer.

The realloc( ) Function

Say you wish to change the length of an array after data has already been placed in it. If you attempt to use malloc( ) to adjust an array to a larger size, you'll gain a larger array, but you'll also lose all data that already exists in that array.

The realloc( ) function will assist you in this situation. It has two parameters: a pointer and an amount of memory. This function reserves the appropriate amount of memory, copying all contents of the old variable into it. This function returns a pointer to the new array. Figure 13-4 contains an example of the use of realloc( ).

Figure 13-4. The realloc( ) Function in Context

```c
#include <stdio.h>
#include <alloc.h>

main()
{
  int *d;
  int i;

  d = malloc(10 * sizeof(int));
  if (!d)
    exit(1);
  for ( i=0; i<10; i++ )
    d[i] = i*i;
  printf("%d\n",d[5]);
  d = realloc(d, 20 * sizeof(int));
  if (!d)
    exit(1);
  for (i=10; i<20; i++)
    d[i] = i*i;
  printf("%d %d\n",d[5],d[15]);
}
```

Note that some new statements have been added. Because most machines have limited memory, malloc( ) and realloc( ) cannot guarantee that space will be available. If these functions cannot reserve the correct amount of memory, they return null. You should always check the return from these functions. If you attempt to use a null pointer, you'll crash the machine.

In Figure 13-4, the pointer is checked to see if it's null. If it is, then no space was reserved, and the program exits gracefully with exit(1).

Pointers can be used as parameters to functions just like arrays. In fact, when you attempt to pass an array as a parameter, the compiler automatically changes that parameter to a pointer. Thus, if you have the function declaration

add(int a[10])

C converts this to

add(const int *a)

This explains many of the strange occurrences when you use an array parameter. The const keyword will be described later. It's used to prevent the value of a variable from changing.

Even though the compiler allows you to pass arrays as parameters, you should always use pointers instead. This makes the conversion more obvious and reduces the likelihood that you'll make a mistake.

It's possible to use pointers to point to other variables. In such a case, the pointer operator allows you to look at the value pointed to by the pointer variable, which is the contents of the other variable. Figure 13-5 provides an example of this.

Figure 13-5. Looking at a Variable Through Use of a Pointer

```
main()
{

    int a,*b;
    a = 5;
    b = &a;                 /* b now points to a */
    printf("%d\n",*b);      /* Prints 5 */
    *b = 4;                 /* Changes a to 4 */
    printf("%d\n",a);       /* Prints 4 */

}
```

This may be useful at times, but it might create a problem. You can now change the value of the variable a without actually using its name. Not only does this make the program more difficult to understand but some compilers perform an optimization that causes such constructs to fail. Thankfully *Turbo C* won't perform this optimization unless you explicitly tell it to do so.

As you can see, pointers can be dangerous unless they're used with care. They're also very powerful. As you'll see in the second part of this book, pointers allow you to access all portions of the IBM PC directly. The next chapter will describe that last major type operator in C, *structures,* and will describe how each of these operators interacts with the others. You'll learn how to create an array of pointers or a pointer to an array.

Chapter 14

Structures

Arrays allow you to tie a number of variables of the same type to a single name. *Structures* allow you tie a number of variables of *different* types together under a single name. This allows you to handle large groups of related data in parameter lists or assignment statements.

To declare a structure, you use the word *struct* followed by an optional *tag,* a block containing standard variable declarations, and a list of variable names. Each of these variables then will contain all of the variables listed in the block. Figure 14-1 contains an example of a simple structure.

Figure 14-1. A Simple Structure

```
main()
{

struct employee
{
  int id;
  char name[80];
  float earnings;
  char *comments;
} employee1, employee2;


}
```

As you can see, a structure can contain any legal C declaration including pointers and arrays. Figure 14-1 creates two variables, employee1 and employee2.

Using a Tag

If you've used a tag in the declaration, you can create more variables of the same type by using the tag name and omitting the block as shown in the line below. The original declaration of this structure must appear before this declaration.

struct employee employee3, employee4;

The period (.) is the structure member operator. It allows you to access each of the members of the structure by name. The name of any element of a structure is the variable name followed by a period and the member name. Figure 14-2 shows how the employee structure might be used.

Figure 14-2. Using the Structure Operator

```
employee1.id = 109;
strcpy(employee1.name,"STEVE");
employee1.earnings = 1431.24;
employee1.comments = "Consider a raise";
```

Each structure member can be treated as if it were a standard variable. It may be passed as a parameter, used in an expression or printed just as if it were a normal variable of the appropriate type.

You can also manipulate a structure as a single object. In *Turbo C,* you may assign one structure to another as in Figure 14-3.

Figure 14-3. Assigning One Structure to Another

```
employee1.id = 106;
employee2 = employee1;
printf("%d\n",employee2.id);
```

Note that this isn't available in some earlier versions of C. In those versions of C, you have to use memcpy( ) as you did with arrays. If you intend to make your *Turbo C* programs portable to other environments, you should avoid structure assignments.

Comparing Structures

Unfortunately, you can't compare structures with the comparison operators. However, as the previous example implied, structure names actually are pointers, and they can be used as pointers. To compare two structures, you can use the memcmp( ) function. This takes two pointers and a number of bytes. It then compares the data pointed to by these pointers. If both sets of data are identical over that number of bytes, zero is returned. (Note: This is an odd function; it returns FALSE for success.) Otherwise, a nonzero value is returned. Figure 14-4 contains an example.

Figure 14-4. Using memcmp( )

```
if (!memcmp(employee3,employee4,sizeof(struct employee)))
   printf("These employees are identical!\n");
```

Note that there's a similar function called strcmp( ) that works with null-terminated character strings.

Structures as Parameters

Structures can also be used as parameters to functions. This is another place where the structure tag is important. You wouldn't want to have to list the entire declaration for each structure parameter. As you saw before, the *struct tag* can replace the actual structure definition if the tag has been previously declared. Figure 14-5 shows a function that uses a structure as a parameter.

Figure 14-5. A Function that Uses a Structure as a Parameter

```
struct employee
{
  int id;
  char name[80];
  float earnings;
  char *comments;
} employee1, employee2;


void print_employee(struct employee emp1)
{
```

```
    printf("Records for %s\n",emp1.name);
    printf("employee %d\n",emp1.id);
    printf("\n%s earned $%f\n",emp1.name,emp1.earnings);
    printf(emp1.comments);
}

void main()
{
}
```

Using Structure, Array, and Pointer Operators

Structure, array, and pointer operators can all be used together in a single variable declaration. The effect of combining these operations isn't always clear. For example, what is created by this declaration?

int *test[10];

Is this an array of ten integer pointers or a pointer to an array of ten integers? To determine this, you must look at the precedence of each of these operators.

The array operator has a higher precedence, so it's the first one bound to test. Thus test becomes an array of ten integers. The pointer operator then makes each integer a pointer to an integer, creating an array of ten integer pointers.

To create a pointer to an array of ten integers, you must change the precedence with parentheses. The pointer operator should be bound to the variable first as follows:

int (*test)[10];

Figure 14-6 contains some examples of these mixed operators.

Figure 14-6. Mixed Operators and Their Meanings

Operators	Meanings
int *test[10];	An array of ten int pointers
int (*test)[10];	A pointer to an array of ten ints
int (*test[10])[10];	An array of ten arrays of ten int pointers
struct employee *test;	A pointer to an employee structure
struct employee test[10];	An array of ten employee structures
struct employee (*test)[10];	A pointer to an array of ten employee structures
int **test;	A pointer to a pointer to an int

The typedef Declaration

As you can see, declarations can become complicated. In order to prevent multiple copies of these complicated definitions, C provides the typedef declaration. When this declaration precedes any standard variable declaration, that declaration becomes a type declaration instead. The new type then may be used to declare new variables. See Figure 14-7.

Figure 14-7. Using the typedef Command

```
main()
{

int test;            /* test is an integer variable */

typedef int test1;   /* Test1 is now a type */

test1 test2;    /* Test2 is now of type test1 (int) */

typedef float *((* strange)[10])[20];

                     /* Type strange is a pointer to an array
                        of 20 arrays of floats */

strange weird;  /* The variable weird is of type strange
                        (a pointer to a pointer to an array of 20 arrays
                        of ten floats) */
}
```

The typdef declaration can be used with any legal type. It can greatly improve the readability of a program. It would be easy to misplace a bracket or parenthesis if you had to use the entire declaration of strange every time a new variable of that type were declared. When this type is given a single name (usually in a header file), it's far easier to deal with.

Pointers to Structures

Pointers to structures deserve special mention. Experienced C programmers often use such pointers. Unfortunately, accessing a member is a little odd, as you can see in Figure 14-8.

Figure 14-8. Accessing a Member of a Structure via a Pointer

```
(*employee).id = 109;
strcpy((*employee).name,"Steve");
```

C provides the -> operator as a shortcut to this operation. The -> operator performs the same operation on a structure pointer as the period (.) performs on a structure. Figure 14-9 shows how this is used.

Figure 14-9. Using the -> Operator

```
employee->id = 109;
strcpy(employee->name,"Steve");
```

The designers of C provided this operator to encourage programmers to pass a structure pointer to procedures rather than the entire structure. When you pass a value as a parameter, C makes an entirely new copy of this value. If that value is a structure, it will consume a large amount of memory. By passing a pointer instead, you use only as much memory as the pointer requires, usually four bytes. Figure 14-10 shows a structure passed as a pointer.

Figure 14-10. A Structure Passed as a Parameter

```
typedef struct employee emp;

void print_employee(emp *emp1)
{
        printf("Records for %s",emp 1->name);
        printf("Employee %d\n",emp 1->id);
        printf("\n%s earned $%g\n",emp 1->name,emp 1->earnings);
        printf(emp 1->comments);

}

main()
{
    emp steve;        /*NOT a pointer!*/

    steve.id  = 109
    strcpy(steve_name,"Steve");
    steve.earned = 1021.212;
    steve.comments = "Goofs off too much";
    print_employee(&steve);  /* Pass the address */

}
```

The passing of pointers rather than structures has two implications. First, because you aren't passing the structure, C doesn't have to make a new copy of that structure on the stack. Second, because you aren't creating a new copy of the structure, any changes you make to the structure still will be in effect when the function ends. If the entire structure is passed, any changes will be in effect only inside the function. As you can see, C provides great flexibility in its data structures. While these operations may seem complicated at first, with some practice, you'll soon come to appreciate their power.

The use of some of these structures may not be obvious at this point, but in the second half of this book you'll see them at work, and their purpose will be made clear.

Chapter 15

Macro Functions

Three lines is generally agreed to be the minimum length for a function. If functions are shorter than three lines, the PC will actually spend more time calling functions than executing the statements in the functions. There are times, however, when you have a complicated one- or two-line expression that you'd prefer to make into a function for the sake of clarity. Suppose you had to repeat the expression

$a + 41*(c/5) - 32$

30 times in a single program. Then further suppose that you needed to change the constant 32 to 31. You'd have to change this number in 30 places. The expression stays the same, so you could use a macro. All you'd need to do is say

#define MYFUNC $a + 41*(c/5) - 32$

But what if you don't always use *a* and *c* as variables? What if you plug different numbers into the formula at different places. Are you forced to drop macros? Not at all. You can use a *macro function*.

Like a C function, a macro function takes parameters. Unlike a C function, a call to a macro function is replaced by the macro definition when the program is compiled. Figure 15-1 contains a simple macro function.

Figure 15-1. A Simple Macro Function

```
#include <stdio.h>
#define MYFUNC(x,y) ((x)+41*((y)/5)-32)

main()
{
        int a=1,b,c=-3;

        b = MYFUNC(a,c);
        printf("The value is %d\n",b);

}
```

Note that the macro name contains a parameter list. Unlike standard C functions, this parameter list contains no type operators. Macro functions ignore types. Also, the name of the macro definition shouldn't contain any spaces. If there were a space between *MYFUNC* and *(X,Y)*, for example, the compiler would assume that you wanted a macro called MYFUNC and were defining it as (X,Y). This would produce very strange results.

As with simple macros, the definition replaces the name as the program is compiled. The variables are replaced with the values placed inside the parentheses in the call. The preprocessor would convert the program in Figure 15-1 to the text in Figure 15-2 before compiling it.

Figure 15-2. The Preprocessor's Interpretation of the Function in Figure 15-1

```
main()
{
  int a=1,b,c=-3;

  b = ((a)+41*((c)/5)-32);
  printf("The value is %d\n",b);
}
```

Note that the variables *a* and *c* replace the variables X and Y in the macro definition.

Macro functions can be very handy, but they also have some traps associated with them. In the previous example, parentheses were placed around the variables X and Y. This may seem unnecessary. However, these parentheses can prevent a bug that's very hard to catch. Consider the program in Figure 15-3.

Figure 15-3. Failure to Separate Parameters with Parentheses Can Create Bugs

```
#include <stdio.h>
#define MYFUNC(x,y)  (x*2+(y*2)+10)

main()
{

        int a=2,b,c=-3;

        b = MYFUNC(a+3,c);
        printf("The value is %d\n",b);

}
```

Nothing's wrong with this, right? Run it. What answer do you get? When you plug 5 and −3 into the equation, you should get 14, right? Why does the computer print 12? Consider what happens when the macros are evaluated. The program in Figure 15-4 is created.

Figure 15-4. How the Preprocessor Interprets the Program Above

```
main()
{
  int a=2,b,c=-3;

  b = (a+3*2+(c*2)+10);
  printf("The value is %d\n",b);
}
```

Now evaluate the above expression. Remember that multiplication takes precedence over addition. The parameter a + 3 wasn't evaluated before being placed into the expression, so the multiplication is performed before the addition. The easiest way to avoid such bugs is to use parentheses as in Figure 15-5.

Figure 15-5. Parentheses Eliminate Ambiguity in Macro Functions

```
#include <stdio.h>
#define MYFUNC(x,y)  ((x)*2+((y)*2)+10)

main()
{
        int a=2,b,c=-3;

        b = MYFUNC(a+3,c);
        printf("The value is %d\n",b);

}
```

The result of this function will be 14 because the preprocessor converts the program to the code in Figure 15-6.

Figure 15-6. The Preprocessor's Interpretation of the Previous Function

```
main()
{
  int a=2,b,c=-3;

  b = ((a+3)*2+((c)*2)+10);
  printf("The value is %d\n",b);
}
```

Because the a + 3 is in parentheses, it's performed before
the multiplication.

The other major trap involving macros concerns any operator that modifies the contents of a variable. The
autoincrement operator is a prime example. Consider the
program in Figure 15-7.

Figure 15-7. The Autoincrement Operator and the Macro Function

```
#include <stdio.h>
#define SQUARE(X)          ((X)*(X))


main()
{

        int a=5;



        printf("Five squared is %d\n",SQUARE(a++));
        printf("This should be six:%d\n",a);



}
```

Looks logical, doesn't it? But what does the preprocessor do to this? Look at Figure 15-8.

Figure 15-8. The Preprocessor's Interpretation of the Preceding Function

```
#include <stdio.h>

main()
{
  int a=5;

  printf("Five squared is %d\n",((a++)*(a++)));
  printf("This should be six:%d\n",a);
}
```

You didn't mean to increment the variable a twice, did you? To make matters worse, the result of incrementing a variable twice in an expression isn't clear. Some compilers will perform the increment after the expression is evaluated, others (*Turbo C* included) will perform the increment after the variable is used.

Incrementing inside of a macro can be even worse. Consider Figure 15-9.

Figure 15-9. Incrementing Within a Macro

```
#include <stdio.h>
#define ADD_ONE(X)          (X++);


main()
{

        int a=4;

        ADD_ONE(a);

        printf("a is %d, 5+1 is %d\n",a,ADD_ONE(5));



}
```

This program won't compile. Superficially, it looks correct. By the preprocesser converts this to Figure 15-10.

Figure 15-10. The Preprocessor's Interpretation of the Function in Figure 15-9

```
#include <stdio.h>


main()
{
   int a=4;

   a++;
   printf("a is %d, 5+1 is %d\n",a,5++);
}
```

What does 5+ + mean? Since 5 is a constant, not a variable, you can't change its value. The compiler will complain that 5 is not an *lvalue*. An lvalue is another word for variable (the exact definition isn't important unless you intend to write a compiler). It never was explicitly stated, but any operator that changes the value of a variable cannot be used on a constant.

What's less obvious is that a function call isn't an lvalue either. Thus, getch( )+ + would also generate a compiler error. It wouldn't add 1 to the value read.

If you avoid the dangerous operators in macro functions, you shouldn't have any problems. The dangerous operators include + +, − −, and all of the assignment operators. In general, however, macro functions can be very useful. If you have doubts as to how a macro is evaluating, use CPP to compile your program. It will show you exactly what the preprocessor is doing.

Chapter 16

Type Modifiers

There are times when you must modify the way the compiler treats variables. This is done with a number of type-modifying keywords. Each keyword must precede a legal variable declaration.

Register

The simplest of the type modifiers is the *register* keyword. If you wish, you can ignore this modifier completely, because it has no effect on how the program runs. The register keyword can affect the program's efficiency, however. When you precede a variable declaration with register, *Turbo C* will attempt to store that variable's data in a machine register rather than at a memory address as it does with normal variables. Register accesses are always faster than memory accesses, so this will cause the program to execute faster. Of course, the 8086 only has 2–4 registers available at any one time, so the number of such variables is limited. If the compiler cannot find an available register, it will place the variable in memory.

Because *register variables* have no addresses, they aren't as flexible as normal variables. You cannot, for example, use the & operator to find their addresses. This means that you cannot pass such a variable to a function by pointer as some functions require   scanf( ), for example.

Register variables are most often used as loop control variables. You rarely use the address of such variables and because they're accessed so often, great time savings can be gained by using registers to store their values. Figure 16-1 contains an example.

Figure 16-1. Using a Register Variable as a Loop Counter

```
#include <stdio.h>


main()
{

      register int i;

      for ( i=0; i<10; i++ )
            printf("Hello!\n");



}
```

Const and Volatile

The const and volatile modifiers are used to help offset the problem compilers can have with pointers when they attempt to optimize code. The const modifier prevents any modification to a variable. A pointer declared as const cannot be modified, but what it points to can be.

As you recall, some compilers (including *Turbo C,* if you specify the -Z option) assume that a variable isn't changed if the program never explicitly changes it. This can cause problems if the variable is changed through the use of a pointer.

The *volatile* keyword helps solve this problem. It tells the compiler that the variable it modifies could change at any moment. The compiler will then avoid optimizing code concerning that variable.

Figure 16-2 has an example of this keyword in use.

Figure 16-2. Using the Volatile Keyword

```
#include <stdio.h>


main()
{
        volatile int a;

        int *b;
        b = &a;
        a = 5;
        *b = 7;
        printf("   a is %d\n");



}
```

Note that in *Turbo C*, this example will work with or without the volatile keyword. Other compilers may not be so well behaved. If you intend to write portable code, you should use volatile in such situations.

In *Turbo C*, the main use of the volatile modifier is with interrupt routines. These will be described more fully later, but the basic concept is that you have a routine in memory that could be called at any time, even in the middle of another routine. If this interrupting routine changes a variable that has been optimized by the compiler, the optimization may cause the correct value to be lost. No compiler could ever be smart enough to optimize in such situations, so volatile should always be used on variables shared by an interrupt and any other function.

Static and Automatic Variables

Normally, the values in variables local to a function are forgotten when the function ends. If you call the function again, such variables will be undefined. These variables are called *automatic variables*. (There's an auto keyword that specifies variables as such, but, because it's the default, it's never necessary.)

It's possible to tell C to save such values as if the variables were global without actually declaring them outside of the function. This is done with the static modifier. Consider Figure 16-3.

Figure 16-3. Use of Static

```
#include <stdio.h>

int i;

void add_one()
{
   static int i=0;

   i++;
   printf("%d\n",i);
}

main()
{
   for ( i=0; i<10; i++ )
     add_one();
}
```

Note that the variable *i* in add_one( ) retains its value when the function ends even though it's declared local to add_one( ). Also notice that this variable doesn't conflict with the global variable *i* even though it acts as if it were global. Try removing the static modifier. Notice that the function can no longer remember the consecutive values of *i*.

Splitting Programs into Separate Files

As mentioned before, it's possible to split a C program into separate files. This is fairly easy. There are a few simple rules to follow:

• No function may be split between two files.
• Prototypes for a function (though not necessarily the accompanying definition) must be present in any file containing calls to that function.
• Any global variable declarations must precede any references to those variables in the same file.

As each file of a C program is compiled, it produces an object file. To create the actual executable version of a program, all of its object files must be combined using another program called a *linker*. In order to correctly link a program, the linker must find definitions for all functions accessed in any of the object modules as well as declarations for all variables used in any module. In addition, the linker must find one function called main( ).

The *Turbo C* compiler automatically runs the *Turbo C* linker after it has finished compiling all C files given it on the command line. Until now, you have always given the compiler a single filename. If your program is made up of a number of files, simply give the compiler all of the filenames. All files then will be compiled, and the resulting object files will be linked together. (The method for handling multiple files in the integrated environment will be described in Chapter 18.)

What does this have to do with variable declarations? Well, there's one problem with the way the linker handles variables. Suppose you want to access a variable declared in another file. If the variable isn't declared in a file that attempts to use it, the compiler will complain that it isn't declared (the compiler looks at one file at a time). If the variable is declared in more than one file, however, the linker will complain that it's declared twice. What can you do?

The extern Modifier

The *extern* type modifier may precede any legal variable declaration. It tells the compiler that a variable exists with the following declaration, but that it's located in another file. This provides the compiler with the declaration it wants. However, it doesn't create the variable. Thus the linker will find only one declaration.

Any variable declared extern should have a matching nonexternal declaration somewhere in the same program (not the same file). The only exception is that the external declaration cannot be initialized. Figure 16-4 contains two files that could be compiled to create a single program.

Figure 16-4. Two Files to Compile into a Single Function

```
/*main.c*/
#include <stdio.h>

extern int a_number;  /*In add_it.c*/
                      /*Note: no initialization*/
int add_it(void);     /*In add_it.c*/

main()
{
  int x;
  x = add_it();
  printf("%d\n",x);
  x = add_it();
  printf("%d\n",x);
}
/*End main.c*/
```

```
/*add_it.c*/
#include <stdio.h>

int a_number = 9;        /*Can be initialized here */

int add_it(void);
```

```
int add_it();
{
  a_number += 10;
  return a_number;
}
/*End add_it.c*/
```

To compile this program, enter *TCC MAIN.C ADD_IT.C* at the DOS prompt. The compiler will compile both C files and then link the resulting object files together. You may come across older C programs that use the extern modifier in function declarations. Originally, prototypes required the extern modifier. This requirement has been dropped. *Turbo C* will allow you to use extern in a prototype, but it will never require it.

Previously, static was used only in the context of local variables. It's possible to declare global variables or functions as static. This will have a slightly different effect on global variables from its effect on local variables.

The word *static* really has two meanings. First, it states that the value in the variable should never be discarded (this has no meaning for static functions). In addition, static states that the variable or function can be seen only in the block in which it's declared.

This second meaning is exactly the inverse of extern. A variable or function declared as static can be used only in the file in which it was declared. Note that such a variable or function still would be seen in every function in that file. Obviously this application of static is less useful.

Functions usually are declared static so that programmers can remind themselves that they're to be used only in that file. *Turbo C* will allow you to call a nonstatic function from a different file even without a prototype. Variables aren't normally seen outside of the current file anyway. Static will take precedence over extern, however. If you've declared a variable as static, it cannot be declared extern anywhere in the program.

Chapter 17

Special Features of C

This chapter describes some of the special features or expressions that are unique to C. None of these features are complex enough to warrant a chapter of their own, but all are important for any C programmer to know.

If you're at all familiar with DOS, you know that some programs allow you to enter arguments after the name of the program. For example, you could type DIR *.C to see a listing of all .C files in the current directory. You might want to use some of these DOS features in C.

The function main( ) can be declared with parameters. These parameters provide information about the arguments entered with the program. This example shows how main( ) can be declared with parameters:

main(int argc, char *argv[ ])

The first parameter, argc will contain the number of space-separated arguments used on the command line. The name of the program is included, thus if you ran the program MY_PROG with the command MY_PROG 1 14, argc would be set to 3.

The second parameter, argv, is an array of pointers to character strings. Each string corresponds to an argument on the command line. If you ran MY_PROG with the command MY_PROG 1 14, *argv[0] would contain MY_PROG, *argv[1] would contain 1 (the string, not the number), and *argv[2] would contain 14.

Figure 17-1 contains a short program that uses this feature.

Figure 17·1. A Program That Utilizes Arguments

```
/*math.c*/

#include <stdio.h>
#include <string.h> /*Contains stricmp()*/
#include <stdlib.h> /*Contains exit()*/
#include <ctype.h>  /*Contains atoi():string to integer convert*/

main(int argc, char *argv[])

{
  if(argc <4)
  {
    printf("Error! Only %d arguments!\n",argc);
    exit(1);

  }
  else /*Not really necessary because of exit()*/
  {
    if(!stricmp(argv[1],"add"))
      printf("%s + %s = %d\n",argv[2],argv[3],atoi(argv[2])+atoi(argv[3]));

    if(!stricmp(argv[1],"subtract"))
      printf("%s - %s = %d\n",argv[2],argv[3],atoi(argv[2])-atoi(argv[3]));

    if(!stricmp(argv[1],"multiply"))
      printf("%s * %s = %d\n",argv[2],argv[3],atoi(argv[2])*atoi(argv[3]));

    if(!stricmp(argv[1],"divide"))
      printf("%s / %s = %d\n",argv[2],argv[3],atoi(argv[2])/atoi(argv[3]));
  }

}
```

This program can be run in the integrated environment, though the method is a little strange. You must first choose the arguments option from the option menu and enter the list of arguments (such as add 2 3). From the command line, you'd simply enter MATH ADD 2 3.

The Conditional Operator

Another feature of C rarely found in other languages is the conditional operator (?). This operator packs the power of an if-then statement into a mathematical expression. This operator operates on three expressions. If the first expression is true, then the second expression is returned; otherwise, the third expression is returned. The syntax of this operator is

expression 1 ? expression 2 : expression 3;

For example, suppose you wanted the value of variable *b* to have the same sign as variable *a*. In other words, make *b* negative if *a* is negative, or make *b* positive if *a* is positive.

This can be done without an if-then statement as shown here:

b = abs(b) * (a < 0 ? −1 : 1);

The expression in the parentheses will return −1 if *a* is less than 0. Otherwise, it will return 1. By multiplying this by the absolute value of *b*, you gain the sign of *a* while retaining the original value of *b*.

This operator is easy to forget, but it can be extremely useful. For example, consider the macro definition below. This definition of MAX( ) can greatly simplify many C programs.

#define MAX(X,Y) ((X)<(Y) ? (X) : (Y))

Without the conditional operator, you'd be forced to use a full if-then statement. The macro immediately above can, on the other hand, be used in almost any C expression.

Bitwise Operators

C also provides a special set of *bitwise* operators. Normally, you think of values in C as integers. These values actually are represented as binary numbers. It's possible through the use of bitwise operators to manipulate these bits directly.

There are four bitwise operators: and (&), or (|), exclusive or (∧), and not (˜). Note that three of these operators have Boolean counterparts: and (&&), or (‖), and not (!).

The difference between the bitwise operators and their Boolean equivalents is that the Boolean operators operate on a value as a whole, while bitwise operators operate on each bit individually. For example, the & operator compares the first bit in each value. If both are true, it sets the first bit in the result to TRUE. Otherwise, it sets the first bit in the result to FALSE. In either case, it moves on to the next bit, performing the same test again. The && operator compares two values as a whole. If both values are the same, it returns a logical TRUE (1); otherwise, it returns a logical FALSE (0).

Thus & will set a bit in the result only if the corresponding bits in the operands are true. The or operator (|) will set a bit if either of the corresponding bits in the operands are true. The exclusive-or operator (∧) will set a bit if one and only one of the corresponding bits in the operands is true. The not operator (˜) will set all bits to 1 that are 0 in the operand and will set to 0 all those that are 1.

These operators should be used only with unsigned numbers. Their effect on signed numbers can be a little strange. Usually this won't be a problem as these operators are usually used in very machine-specific ways, as you'll see later in this book.

Assignment operators exist that correspond to three of the bitwise operators. These are &=, |=, and ∧=. Like the + = operator, these operators combine an operation and an assignment in one step. For instance, the expression

a &= b;

is the equivalent of

a = a & b;

A final pair of bitwise operators shifts binary values right or left a specified number of places. For example, 11011101 shifted to the right two places would become 00110111 (characters that "fall off the end" are lost, and zeros are shifted in as needed). The first operand is the value to be shifted, the second is the number of digits to shift. The left-shift operator is < <, and the right-shift operator is > >.

You should beware of using the shift operators with signed numbers. Unpredictable results will occur if you shift negative numbers to the right or large positive numbers to the left. Most of the problems will disappear if you first cast the values as an unsigned type.

Because of the way binary arithmetic works, the shift operators provide a very fast way of multiplying or dividing by powers of 2. For example, the expression 3 < < 2 produces

12. The expression 3 < < 2 is equivalent to 3 * (2∧2). Shift operations are far more efficient than regular multiplication, so if speed is crucial, these operators should be used wherever possible.

Another somewhat odd operator in C is the comma operator (,). The result of this operation is always the rightmost value listed. For example, the expression a = (2,3,4) evaluates to 4. (The parentheses are necessary because the comma operator has a lower precedence than the assignment operator.) This seems like a perfectly useless operator. You may wonder why anyone would want to evaluate an expression and then throw it away. Well, you've seen it already. Consider this for loop:

for (i=0,j=0; j<9 && i<9; i+ +,j+ +)

The comma operator is used twice: once to fit two assignments into the initial conditions (only one expression is allowed) and once to fit two increments in the repeated statement section (again, only one expression is allowed).

The Union

C also provides a special type of structure called a *union*. A union allows you to give an area of memory more than one name. It's declared just like a structure (also called a *struct*). Unlike a structure, however, each of its members will occupy the same space in memory. Figure 17-2 contains a simple union declaration.

Figure 17-2. Use of the Union

```
union multi
{
   int a,b;
   char c;
};


void main()
{
}
```

In this declaration, *a, b,* and *c* will all begin at the same memory location. If you assign a value to multi.a, it will appear in multi.b and in multi.c. There's no restriction against different types sharing memory. In Figure 17-2, the one-byte variable *c* will share the top byte of the two-byte variables *a* and *b*.

The primary use of unions is that they can allow you to convert between types. Suppose, for example, that you needed to split integer values into their character components. The union declaration in Figure 17-3 would help you accomplish this.

Figure 17-3. The Union In Context

```
union convert
{
  int integer;
  char character[2];
} to_convert;
```

To break an integer into its two one-byte components, you'd use the assignment

to_convert.integer = x;

The characters then could be removed with assignments like

high = to_convert.character[0]
low = to_convert.character[1];

Bitfields

Until now, C hasn't allowed you direct access to the individual bits that make up a byte. When space is critical, it can be useful to reserve only a single bit for use as a variable. C allows you to do this to a limited extent with *bitfields*.

Bitfields always must be structure members and always must be integers. A bitfield is declared by appending a colon and an integer value to a structure-member declaration. See Figure 17-4.

Figure 17-4. Use of the Bitfield

```
struct bits
{
    unsigned one:1;      /* 0..1 */
    unsigned three:3;    /* 0..8 */
    unsigned twelve:12;  /* 0..2^12 */
}
```

The compiler will take the above declaration and pack it into as small a space as possible. It must, however, follow some rules of its own. It must only use multiples of 16 bits and it can't create arrays of bitfields or pointers to bitfields. Bitfields cannot be used as parameters.

The space occupied by a set of bitfields is always rounded up to the nearest multiple of 16 bits. Thus, it makes little sense to declare only a single bitfield. Bitfields should always come in groups.

Bitfields, with some minor restrictions, can be used like any other variables. Bitfields are assigned and operated on as normal integers. Care must be taken, however, when assigning values to bitfields as they usually have a much smaller range.

Also note that while bitfields are part of standard C, many implementations only allow unsigned bitfields. This is only a concern if you intend to port your programs to other machines.

The enumerated Type

A final interesting feature of C is the *enumerated type*. The easiest way to think of an enumerated type is as an extension of macros. You declare an enumerated type by giving a variable a list of names. C then automatically assigns a series of values to the named variables. This may sound a little odd, but the next two figures should make it clear for you. Figure 17-5 contains a simple example of the enumerated type.

Figure 17-5. Use of the enumerated Type

```
enum days {mon, tue, wed, thu, fri, sat, sun};
enum days day;
```

This creates an integer variable called day and assigns numbers to the days listed above. It's functionally equivalent to the code in Figure 17-6.

Figure 17-6. The Equivalent Routine Without Recourse to enumerated Type

```
int day;
#define mon 0
#define tue 1
#define wed 2
#define thu 3
#define fri 4
#define sat 5
#define sun 6
```

Both constructs would allow statements such as

day = wed;

Note that the definitions created by the enum statement aren't truly macros. You can only use them with the declared variables.

You can explicitly assign values to names in an enum statement simply by assigning that value to name. Figure 17-7 shows a simple example of this.

Figure 17-7. Using enumerated Type with Names

```
enum employees {Kris=100, Jim=103, Robin=104, Larry=107,
Steve=109};
enum employees employee = Steve;
```

The advantage of enumerated types is that these definitions are used only with variables declared as enumerated
types. This helps prevent errors caused by accidental text
substitution as shown in figure 17-8.

Figure 17-8. An Error That Might Be Avoided with enumerated Types

```
#define Steve 109
int Steve, employee;    /* Bad!: int 109, employee; */

employee = Steve;       /* Ok: employee = 109; */
Steve = 1;              /* Bad!: 109 = 1; */
```

It should be noted that enumerated types are a fairly recent addition to C. If you move to an older version of C,
they may not be available.

This chapter concludes the description of the C language. All of the programs will work with any standard C
compiler. The next two chapters describe two special *Turbo C*
facilities: project management and in-line assembly.

Chapter 18

Projects and the Make Facility

C allows programs to be broken into separate files. Unfortunately, it can be tedious to compile every file that makes up a program every time a change is made in one of them. If you have ten C files, the compiler must compile all ten. What if only one was changed?

You don't actually have to recompile all ten. Whenever you compile a file, C leaves an object file (with the suffix .OBJ) in the current directory. If the corresponding C file hasn't been changed, you can use this object file to create the program without recompiling. For example, suppose you compiled a program made up of five files with the command TCC MAIN.C A.C B.C C.C D.C. You then discover you need to change A.C. Using the previous command, you'd cause *Turbo C* to recompile all five source files.

To avoid recompiling unchanged files, use the object file in place of the C file. The previous command would then become TCC MAIN.OBJ A.C B.OBJ C.OBJ D.OBJ. Only A.C would be recompiled.

Unfortunately, to do this, you have to keep track of which files make up a program and which files have changed. Using the project facility in the integrated environment, you can avoid this. You simply create a file listing all of the files in your program and give this name to the integrated environment. From then on, the compiler will compile only those files that have changed since the last compilation.

For example, to compile the previous program, you'd first create the project file PROG.PRJ as in Figure 18-1.

Figure 18·1. PROJ.PRJ File

main.c
a.c
b.c
c.c
d.c

Next, you'd assign the project name to PROG.PRJ using the project menu. From then on, you compile as you did with only one file. When you hit Alt-R, *Turbo C* will automatically compile the files that need compiling, link them all together, and run the resulting program.

If your program uses the include directive to include other source files (such as header files), your project file may not work as well as you'd like. If you change a header file that is included in one of your C files, the project facility won't know to recompile the C file. Adding the header filename to the project file won't make matters any better, either. In this case, Turbo C will attempt to compile the header only.

Fortunately, there's a solution. A project file is really a list of dependencies. A file depends on another if it wouldn't exist unless the other file exists. For instance, an object file is dependent on the C file that is used to create it. An executable file depends on the object files used to create it.

The project facility knows these rules. If a C file includes other files, then the object file it creates depends on both the C file and the included files. To tell *Turbo C* this, you must place the names of the included files in parentheses after the filename. Figure 18-2 contains an example of this.

Figure 18·2. Informing *Turbo C* of Dependent Relationships Among Files

main.c   (main.h)
a.c   (main.h, a.h)
b.c   (main.h, b.h)
c.c   (main.h)
d.c   (a.h)

Changing one of the C files will have the same effect as before; *Turbo C* will compile only that C file. Changing one of the header files would cause *Turbo C* to compile one or more of the C files. For example, changing A.H would cause *Turbo C* to recompile A.C and D.C. Changing MAIN.H would cause *Turbo C* to recompile all of the C files except D.C.

The project facility is very powerful, but it may be used only in the integrated environment. The command line version of *Turbo C* has an equally powerful program called MAKE. Users of UNIX will instantly recognize this as a standard UNIX make utility. Unfortunately, MAKE has a structure completely different from the project facility.

MAKE doesn't normally know about dependencies. You have to list them for each file. MAKE always looks for a file in the current directory called *makefile*. This is the default name that MAKE looks for; it contains the list of dependencies. The syntax is also different. Each file occupies at least two lines. The first line contains a filename, a colon, and a list of files on which that file depends. The next few lines contain the commands used to create the file from the files it depends on. A tab must be placed before each command. Figure 18-3 contains a makefile corresponding to the previous project file. To use it to compile a program, you'd simply type *MAKE* on the command line.

Figure 18-3. Sample makefile

```
main.exe          : main.obj a.obj b.obj c.obj d.obj
        tcc main.obj a.obj b.obj d.obj

main.obj      :        main.c main.h
        tcc -c main.c

a.obj   :        a.c main.h
        tcc -c a.c

b.obj   :        b.c main.h b.h
        tcc -c b.c

c.obj   :        c.c main.h
        tcc -c b.c

d.obj   :        d.c a.h
        tcc -c d.c
-
```

The previous example used only explicit rules. MAKE was given a rule for each separate file. It can be given implicit rules such as

All .C files can be converted to .OBJ files using TCC

as in Figure 18-4.

Figure 18-4. Using Implicit Rules with MAKE

```
# <-- Comment marker
# Makefile
.c.obj:
        tcc -c $<

.obj.exe:
        tcc $<

main.exe        :       main.obj a.obj b.obj c.obj d.obj
       tcc main.obj a.obj b.obj d.obj

main.obj        :       main.h

a.obj   :       main.h

b.obj   :       main.h b.h

c.obj   :       main.h

d.obj   :       a.h
```

The pound symbol (#) turns the current line into a comment as shown in the first two lines of this file. The next two lines are the implicit rule. .C.OBJ simply says that all .OBJ files depend on a .C file with the same name. The next line contains the command to convert a .C file to a .OBJ file. The symbol $< represents the name of the file.

You can use MAKE to compile programs not defined in the makefile. For example, if you type MAKE TEST.EXE, MAKE will use the rules it knows to compile that file. If it has no rules concerning the creation of a file, it will look in the current directory for that file. Typing *MAKE TEST.EXE* would cause MAKE to create TEST.EXE. It has no explicit rules for creating TEST.EXE, but it has an implicit rule that any .EXE file can be created from a .OBJ file with the command TCC *file*. It also knows that any .OBJ file can be created from a .C file using the command TCC -C *file*. Using these commands, it creates TEST.EXE from TEST.C.

If you just type *MAKE*, MAKE will try to create all of the programs that it knows about. If you type *MAKE* followed by a filename, it will create only that program. For example, MAKE MAIN.OBJ would only create MAIN.OBJ, not MAIN.EXE. This allows you to add definitions for several programs in a single makefile. Then you can either compile all programs with one command or compile only a single program, or even a piece of a single program.

MAKE also allows you to define macros containing often-used commands. For example, suppose you used ten different flags every time you compiled. You could place the entire command in a macro. You do this simply by assigning the string to a name. To use the macro, you place it in parentheses and precede it with a dollar sign. Figure 18-5 contains a program that uses a macro.

Figure 18-5. Using MAKE with Macros

```
# Makefile
CC = tcc -ms -w -w-sus -Z -O -K
.c.obj:
        $(CC) -c $<

.obj.exe:
        $(CC) $<

main.exe        :        main.obj a.obj b.obj c.obj d.obj
        $(CC) main.obj a.obj b.obj d.obj

main.obj        :        main.h

a.obj   :       main.h

b.obj   :       main.h b.h

c.obj   :       main.h

d.obj   :       d.h a.h
```

When this makefile is processed, the string *$(CC)* will be replaced with *TCC -MS -W W-SUS -Z -O -K.* This saves you a great deal of typing.

A final feature of the *Turbo C* MAKE facility that isn't available in most versions of MAKE is the ability to use compiler directives. These directives work in a manner identical to those used in a program source file. The only difference is that MAKE directives must begin with an exclamation point (!) rather than a pound sign (#). This allows you to place multiple versions of a program in a single makefile as in Figure 18-6.

Figure 18-6. Multiple Versions of a Program in a Single makefile

```
# Makefile
CC = tcc -ms -w -w-sus -DNET=COMPNET -Z -O -K
.c.obj:
        $(CC) -c $<

.obj.exe:
        $(CC) $<

!if COMPNET

main.exe        :       main.obj a.obj b.obj c.obj d.obj net.obj
        $(CC) main.obj a.obj b.obj d.obj net.obj

net.obj :       net.asm
        masm net.asm

!else

main.exe        :       main.obj a.obj b.obj c.obj d.obj net.obj
        $(CC) main.obj a.obj b.obj d.obj net.obj

!endif

main.obj        :       main.h

a.obj   :       main.h

b.obj   :       main.h b.h

c.obj   :       main.h

d.obj   :       d.h a.h
```

The -D option of MAKE allows you to define a macro from the command line. If you used the command MAKE -DCOMPNET = 1, MAKE would add the file NET.OBJ to the definition of MAIN.EXE. In addition, because the -D option of TCC also lets you define macros, all programs would be compiled with the definition NET set to 1.

If you compiled the program using MAKE - DCOMPNET = 0, NET.OBJ wouldn't be included in MAIN.EXE, and all files would be compiled with NET set to 0.

In all respects, these makefile directives act in an identical manner to the compiler directives described in Chapter 7. You should refer to that chapter for more information.

As you can see, the command line MAKE facility is very powerful. Few programmers use even a fraction of its full potential. The project facility in the integrated environment, while less powerful, is much easier to use. It's assumed that programmers using the integrated environment are more interested in ease of use, while those operating from the command line are more likely to want the full power of MAKE.

Chapter 19

In-Line Assembly

As any C programmer will tell you, C provides almost all of the power of machine language in a high-level language. There will come a time, however, when you'll need more than just *almost all* of the power; you'll need machine language. This chapter is meant for programmers who have used machine language. If you don't know 8086 machine language programming, then you should skip this chapter for the time being and make a mental note that you'll have to study it later. (A text you might want to consider is *COMPUTE!'s Beginner's Guide to Machine Language on the IBM PC & PCjr.*) Later chapters won't assume that you know machine language.

Most C compilers require you to put all machine language instructions in separate files. These files must be assembled separately and then linked later. This isn't a convenient process, especially if you only want to use a single machine language instruction.

Turbo C allows you to place machine language instructions anywhere that you'd place a legal C statement. The *asm* keyword signals that the next statement is a machine language instruction. Figure 19-1 shows a function that uses some machine language instructions.

Figure 19-1. Embedding Machine Language in a C Language Program

```
#pragma inline

void popstack(void);

main()
{
}


void popstack(void)
{
```

119

```
    int i;

    asm pop cx; asm pop bx
    asm pop ax
    asm pop dx

    for ( i=0; i<10; i++ )
      asm pop si;

}
```

Note that the semicolons at the end of machine language instructions are optional. Also note that multiple machine language instructions can be placed on a single line. *Turbo C* treats a machine language instruction as a legal C statement.

Unfortunately, because in-line machine language uses the Microsoft assembler, you can't compile programs using in-line machine language in the integrated environment. In addition, you must have the Microsoft (or compatible) assembler.

You may use machine language to move values between registers or to move values between memory and a register. Either operand (but not both) in an in-line machine language instruction may be replaced with a legal variable name. Such variables may be global or local. You may even use structure members as an operand. You may not use arrays in in-line machine language instructions, however. Programs using such array references will compile, but the memory element accessed might be incorrect.

Figure 19-2 contains some examples of memory accesses.

Figure 19-2. Memory Access Examples

```
#pragma inline
#include <stdio.h>

int x,t;

typedef struct test
{
   int a,b;

} struct_test;

main()
{
   int i;
   int x = 1,y;
   struct_test str1;

   asm mov ax,x;
   asm mov y,ax;
   printf("y is %d\n",y);

   asm mov t,ax;
   printf("t is %d\n",t);

   asm mov str1.b,ax;
   printf("str1.b is %d\n",str1.b);

}
```

Keep in mind that all machine language programming rules apply. For example, only one operand can be a memory address. In addition, all memory addresses must be determined at compile time. Thus while standard variable and structure operations are legal, array and pointer references (which might use a variable element number) are not.

You aren't allowed to create machine language labels from C, but *Turbo C* allows you to access C labels from machine language. For example, the program in Figure 19-3 tests and jumps conditionally depending on the value in *x*.

Figure 19-3. Accessing a C Language Label from Machine Language

```
#include <stdio.h>

main()
{
   int x=5;

   asm mov ax,x
   asm cmp ax,9
   asm jg label1

   printf("x is less than nine!\n");
   exit(0);

label1:

   printf("x is greater than nine!\n");

}
```

Note that you're only allowed to use jump instructions, such as JG. Branch instructions such as BNE aren't allowed from *Turbo C*.

You may have noticed that when TCC encounters an in-line machine language instruction, it restarts the compilation process from the beginning, invoking the assembler. You can warn TCC of the machine language instructions ahead of time either by placing the compiler directive

#pragma in-line

at the beginning of the file or by using the -B option of TCC. Neither of these are required, but they will save on compilation time.

Turbo C also allows you to use the compiler to translate C programs into assembly language. The compiler normally translates C programs first to assembly language and then to machine language. The -S option from the command line halts this process at the assembly language stage creating a .ASM file rather than a .OBJ file. You may use any text editor to look at and modify these files. *Turbo C* creates standard Microsoft assembly language files so you can use an editor to modify them and then an assembler to create the object files.

This feature is useful because it allows you to see exactly what the compiler is doing. This will improve your knowledge of the language as a whole and will also improve your use of in-line machine language. The rest of this chapter will provide a brief overview of the way C programs are converted to machine language.

How C Programs Are Converted to Machine Language

C is made up of functions, so function calls are very important and need to be handled in an efficient manner. C passes all parameters on the stack. Each function call will be preceded with a series of push statements. Parameters are always pushed in reverse order; the last parameter is pushed first, then the next to the last, and so on. The values in these parameters are accessed using the BP (base pointer) register, so immediately after the function is called, the BP, SI, and DI registers are pushed to the stack; then the SP (stack pointer) is copied to the BP. Thus, [BP + 8] would be the first parameter, [BP + 10] would be the second, and so on.

Turbo C can store local variables in either of two places. The two most heavily used variables, or variables that have the register modifier, are stored in either the SI or the DI register. Other local variables are stored on the stack. Thus [BP − 2] would be the first nonregister local variable, [BP − 4] would be the second, and so on.

Global variables (as well as function declarations) are always accessed with the names given them in C. In order to avoid confusing such names with assembler labels, *Turbo C* always places a single underscore in front of the name. Thus

call _printf

is a call to the printf( ) function.

Figure 19-4 contains a simple C program along with the assembler output it produces. *Turbo C* automatically places line-number comments in the machine language file for easy reference. Take note of the call to add on line 22, the access of the parameter *x* on line 14, the access of the variable *w* on line 7, and the use of the register SI to store the variable *a* on line 8.

Figure 19-4. C Program and Assembly Language Output

```
#include <stdio.h>

int add(int,int);

int add(int x,int y)
{
   int q=1,w=2,e=3,r=4,t=5;
   int a=4,b;

   b = 9;
   a*=b;
   printf("a is %d\n",a);

   a = x;
   b = y;

   return a+b;
}

main()
{
   printf("4+5=%d",add(4,5));
}


nametoasm
_TEXT    segment byte public 'CODE'
```

```
DGROUP    group    _DATA,_BSS
          assume   cs:_TEXT,ds:DGROUP,ss:DGROUP
_TEXT     ends
_DATA     segment word public 'DATA'
_d@       label    byte
_DATA     ends
_BSSsegment word public 'BSS'
_b@       label    byte
_BSSends
_TEXT     segment byte public 'CODE'
; Line 6
_add      proc     near
          pushsi
          pushdi
          pushbp
          mov      bp,sp
          sub      sp,10
; Line 7
          mov      word ptr [bp-10],1
          mov      word ptr [bp-8],2
          mov      word ptr [bp-6],3
          mov      word ptr [bp-4],4
          mov      word ptr [bp-2],5
; Line 8
          mov      si,4
; Line 9
; Line 10
          mov      di,9
; Line 11
          mov      ax,si
          mul      di
          mov      si,ax
; Line 12
          pushsi
          mov      ax,offset DGROUP:_s@
          pushax
          callnear ptr _print
          pop      cx
          pop      cx
; Line 13
; Line 14
          mov      si,word ptr [bp+8]
; Line 15
          mov      di,word ptr [bp+10]
; Line 16
```

```
; Line 17
        mov     ax,si
        add     ax,di
@1:
; Line 18
        mov     sp,bp
        pop     bp
        pop     di
        pop     si
        ret
_addendp
; Line 21
_main   proc    near
; Line 22
        mov     ax,5
        push    ax
        mov     ax,4
        push    ax
        call    near ptr _add
        pop     cx
        pop     cx
        push    ax
        mov     ax,offset DGROUP:_s@+9
        push    ax
        call    near ptr _printf
        pop     cx
        pop     cx
; Line 23
@2:
        ret
_main   endp
_TEXT   ends
_DATA   segment word public 'DATA'
_s@     label   byte
        db      97
        db      32
        db      105
        db      115
        db      32
        db      37
        db      100
        db      10
        db      0
        db      52
        db      43
        db      53
```

```
          db        61
          db        37
          db        100
          db        0
_DATA     ends
_TEXT     segment   byte public 'CODE'
          extrn     _print:near
          extrn     _printf:near
          public    _add
          public    _main
_TEXT     ends
          end
```

Function calls are the most complicated part of any machine language file the compiler creates. All expressions are broken down into fairly simple operations. All control structures are broken into simple tests and branches. Once you understand the way variables are stored, the rest is fairly simple.

With this chapter, you leave the description of the C language. In the next section of this book, you'll see how C is used. Most of the concepts explained in the next section aren't new, but simply examples of how to apply the statements you've already learned. Because C is so powerful, it's common for programmers new to the language to miss important features simply because they never considered the potential of certain statements. For example, the assignment operator (=) can be used to look at any memory address (this will be described more fully later on). Few descriptions of the C language mention this fact, but no description ever disallows such a use of the assignment operator. These features will be described in the next chapter.

Chapter 20
File Handling

Turbo C handles disk files with standard C I/O (input/output) functions. While these functions aren't technically part of the C language, all standard versions of C will feature the functions described in this chapter.

There are two ways to access disk files. The simplest method is the sequential method. A sequential file operates in a fashion similar to the IBM PC console. You send information to a file with a function called fprintf( ). You read information from a file with a function called fscanf( ).

Opening a File

Before you can use these functions, you must open the file. Opening a file creates a special variable of type FILE. This variable is a pointer, which is used by fprintf( ) and fscanf( ) to find the disk file to use. The fopen( ) function takes two parameters: the filename and an access mode. Possible access modes are listed in Figure 20-1.

Figure 20-1. Possible Access Modes

Access Mode	Meaning
"r"	Open old file for reading.
"w"	Create new file for writing.
"a"	Start writing at the end of a file. (Create it if it doesn't exist.)
"r+"	Open an existing file for both reading and writing.
"w+"	Create a new file for both reading and writing.
"a+"	Open an existing file or create a new file for reading and writing at the end.

Don't worry too much about the file types. You'll usually use only the "r" and "w" types. You won't normally read from and write to a sequential file at the same time.

The fopen( ) function returns a value of type FILE (note that this type is uppercase). This value is then passed as the first parameter to fprintf( ) and fscanf( ). If the file was opened for writing, fprintf( ) will print to the end of the file using the standard printf( ) rules. If the file was opened for reading, fscanf( ) will read starting at the beginning of the file using the standard scanf( ) rules.

When you've finished using a file, you must use the fclose( ) function to tell DOS that you're through. This function takes a single FILE pointer as a parameter.

A Sample Program

Figure 20-2 contains a simple program that will create and write to a file, close it, and then open it and read from it again. All file-handling functions are prototyped in
<fcntl.h>.

Figure 20-2. A File-Handling C Program

```
/* file.c */
#include <stdio.h>
#include <fcntl.h>

main()
{
        FILE *my_file;
        int b = 4;
        char *string = "string1";

        my_file = fopen("datafile.dat","w");     /*Open for writing*/

        if(my_file)              /*Don't continue if NULL!*/
        {
                fprintf(my_file,"word1 ");

                fprintf(my_file,"%s ",string);

                fprintf(my_file,"%d ",b);

                fclose(my_file);

                my_file = fopen("datafile.dat","r");

                if(my_file)
                {
```

```
                fscanf(my_file,"%s",string);
                printf("%s\n",string);
        fscanf(my_file,"%s",string);
                printf("%s\n",string);
                fscanf(my_file,"%s",string);
                printf("%s\n",string);
        }
        else
                printf("Error opening for read!\n");
    }
    else
            printf("Error opening for write!\n");
}
```

Note that the program doesn't attempt to use the file returned by fopen( ) if it's NULL. This function returns NULL if it can't open the file. You should never attempt to read from a file that wasn't properly opened.

The program in Figure 20-2 creates a file with three different elements:

word1
string1
4

Run this program and then load the file DATAFILE.DAT into the editor. Note that the words are placed in the file exactly as they would have been written to the screen.

The second half of the program reads the three elements from the file exactly as if they were entered from the keyboard.

The fscanf( ) function reads from the file until it finds a space, exactly as scanf( ) does from the keyboard. These values are then sent to the screen with print( ).

Coordinating fprintf( ) and fscanf( ) can be a little difficult at first. While fprintf( ) will send a string containing large spaces or carriage returns to the file, fscanf( ) will stop reading as soon as it sees either character. Fortunately, C also contains a file version of gets( ). The fgets( ) function is identical to gets( ) except that it reads from a file instead of from the keyboard.

Streams

A *stream* is a file or physical device that you manipulate with
a pointer to a FILE structure (defined in STDIO.H). You may
move only in one direction in a stream. When reading, you
must move sequentially through the file. You can't read anything unless you've read everything that precedes it in the
file. You can't read anything that has already been read without closing and then reopening the stream. Likewise, information, once written with fprintf( ), cannot be changed without reopening the stream.

Turbo C automatically opens five file streams in every
program. These streams are

stdin
stdout
stdprn
stderr
stdaux

You've already used two of these—stdin and stdout. The
function printf( ) acts identically to a call to fprintf( ) using
stdout as the file parameter. The function fscanf( ) acts identically to a call to scanf( ) using stdin as the file parameter.

Stderr is similar to stdout except that anything sent to it
may not be redirected to a file. From the DOS prompt, you
can redirect the output of a program to a file using the great-
er-than symbol (>). All output sent to stdout will be sent to
the file rather than to the screen. Output sent to stderr will
be sent to the screen whether output has been redirected or
not. This file stream is usually used for error messages.

The stdprn and stdaux streams are used to send information to the IBM PC output ports. Stdprn is meant especially for output to printer devices. It will be discussed briefly in
the next chapter. Because these two streams aren't supported
in Microsoft's OS/2 under protected mode and may not be
supported in future versions of MS-DOS, they should be
avoided. In the following chapter, you'll see how data can be
sent to the printer in a more portable manner.

Like any other stream, these five standard streams can be opened and closed. Of course, you'll lose the ability to write to the screen if you close stdout. Closing stdin causes similar problems. DOS limits you to 20 open files at any one time so there may come a time where you'd consider it necessary to close one or more of the standard streams.

Once closed, reopening these files can be difficult. For example, to open any of the streams associated with the screen or keyboard, you'd need to use the string "CON:" in place of a filename.

Turbo C doesn't write to the disk every time you give it a write command. Instead, it sends all output to a special area called a *buffer*. When the buffer becomes full, its contents are written to the disk, emptying the buffer. Because data is written in chunks, your program will run faster. This method is not without its problems, however. For one thing, if your program doesn't exit normally, either because of an error or some other reason (this is especially important in interrupts), the disk file may not be updated correctly. C provides a special function that forces the buffers to be saved to the disk. The fflush( ) function takes a single stream as a parameter. You can use fflush( ) with the standard streams.

As mentioned earlier, fprintf( ) and fscanf( ) can be tricky. Consider the program in Figure 20-3.

Figure 20-3. Use of fprintf( ) and fscanf( )

```
/* file2.c */
#include <stdio.h>
#include <fcntl.h>

main()
{
        FILE *my_file;
        int b = 4;
        char *string = "string1";

        my_file = fopen("datafile.dat","w");      /*Open for writing*/

        if(my_file)              /*Don't continue if NULL!*/
        {
                fprintf(my_file,"%d",1);
```

```
            fprintf(my_file,"%d",2);

            fprintf(my_file,"%d",b);

            fclose(my_file);

            my_file = fopen("datafile.dat","r");

            if(my_file)
            {
                    fscanf(my_file,"%d",&b);
                    printf("%d\n",b);
        fscanf(my_file,"%d",&b);
                    printf("%d\n",b);
                    fscanf(my_file,"%d",&b);
                    printf("%d\n",b);
            }
            else
                    printf("Error opening for read!\n");
    }
    else
            printf("Error opening for write!\n");
}
```

When you run the program in Figure 20-3, it doesn't produce 1, 2, and then 4 as expected but produces 124 three times. Why? Look at DATAFILE.DAT. As you can see, no spaces were placed between the 1, 2, and 4. Because of this, the first fscanf( ) reads this as a single number. The next two times scanf( ) was called, it failed, leaving the original value of *b* unchanged (the end of the file had been reached). The solution to this problem, of course, is to print spaces between the numbers. This is a fairly simple matter:

fprintf("%d"...

becomes

fprintf("%d "...

There are times (as in the case above) where it would be nice to know whether the end of the file was reached. This can be done with a function called feof( ). This function takes a file pointer and returns true if the end of the associated stream has been reached. Figure 20-4 contains an example of this.

Figure 20-4. Using the feof( ) Function

```
/* file3.c */
#include <conio.h>
#include <stdio.h>
#include <fcntl.h>
#define ESC 27
#define CR 13
#define LF 10

main()
{
        FILE *my_file;
        int ch;

        my_file = fopen("datafile.dat","w");    /*Open for writing*/

        if(my_file)
        {
            while(ESC != (ch = getch())) /* Stop when user hits ESC */
                {
                  if(ch == CR)   /* Change carriage returns to linefeeds */
                    ch = LF;
                    printf("%c",ch);
                    fprintf(my_file,"%c",ch);
                }
                fprintf(my_file,"\n");

                fclose(my_file);

                my_file = fopen("datafile.dat","r");

                if(my_file)
                {
                  while(!feof(my_file)) /* Read until the end of the file */
                      {
                            fscanf(my_file,"%c",&ch);
                            printf("%c",ch);
        }
                }
                else
                        printf("Error opening for read!\n");
        }
        else
                printf("Error opening for write!\n");
}
```

135

This program first reads characters from the keyboard until the Esc key is pressed. Note that carriage returns are replaced with linefeeds. This is because the carriage return character won't move the cursor down one line as you might expect. After it has written these characters to a file, it reopens the file, reading all characters and printing them to the screen. Because this program uses the feof( ) function to find the end of the file, the datafile has no size limit. You can place as many characters as you like in it.

The stdin stream treats the end-of-file character a little differently. Obviously, keyboard input can never end. This doesn't mean that this function will never return true for standard input, however. The end of a normal text file is marked with the Control-Z character. If you type this character from the keyboard, this will cause feof( ) to return true until that character is read. This doesn't halt keyboard input.

Random Access Files

The sequential file functions treat disk files as a sequential series of characters. By contrast, random access file functions treat disk files as arrays of characters. You can move backward or forward through a file, write to and read from the same file, and skip portions of the file. The disadvantage of these routines is that they take more care to use properly.

As with the sequential file functions, the file must first be opened. In this case the function is simply called open( ). This function takes two parameters and, optionally, a third. Instead of returning a file pointer, open( ) returns an integer which acts much like a file pointer.

The first parameter to open( ) is the filename. This is a pointer to a character string as in fopen( ). The second parameter is an integer that represents the access mode. The value of this parameter is created by "ORing" together a number of flags (a subset of these is presented in Figure 20-5).

Figure 20-5. Flags "ORed" Together to Produce the Access Mode Parameter

Flag	Meaning
O_RDONLY	Only allow reading from the file
O_WRONLY	Only allow writing to the file
O_RDWR	Allow both reading and writing
O_CREAT	Create the file if it doesn't exist
O_TRUNC	If the file exists, erase it, creating a new version

If the O_CREAT flag is used, you must specify a third parameter giving the access mode to the file. This parameter is created much as the file access mode. In this case, only two flags exist, S_IWRITE and S_IREAD. These two flags specify the access privileges other programs (including the present one) will have after the file is created.

A typical call to the open( ) function might look like one of those in Figure 20-6.

Figure 20-6. A Typical Call to the open( ) Function

```
int fd
fd = open("datafile.dat", O_CREAT | O_RDWR, S_IREAD | S_IWRITE);
fd = open("datafile.dat", O_RDONLY);
```

The first call to the open( ) function will open a file called DATAFILE.DAT for both reading and writing. If the file doesn't exist, open( ) will create it, giving DOS permission to read and to write to the file. The second call to the open( ) function opens the file DATAFILE.DAT for reading only. In this case, the file must exist or open( ) will return −1 to signify an error.

The functions read( ) and write( ) are used to read from and write to a random access file. Both functions take the same parameters: the integer file handle returned by open( ), a pointer to a buffer to read from or store data to, and the number of bytes of data to read or write.

A buffer is simply a section of memory. The buffer can be any size you wish. It could be a single integer or a 64K array. The write( ) function simply writes the specified number of bytes to the disk starting at the beginning address of the buffer. The read( ) function simply reads the specified number of bytes from the disk to the buffer.

But where on the disk do these functions actually read from or write to? They automatically write to a position indicated by a *file pointer*. When a file is first opened, the file pointer always points to the beginning of the file. Any reads and writes occur wherever the pointer indicates. The act of reading and writing automatically moves the file pointer by the number of bytes read or written. In this way, random access files can act like sequential files.

Moving the File Pointer

You can move the file pointer without reading or writing by using the function lseek( ). This function takes three parameters: The first is the file handle. The second is the offset or the number of bytes to move the pointer (if this number is negative, the pointer will be moved backwards in the file). The third parameter tells lseek( ) the starting location of the move.

Three flags specify starting positions. SEEK_SET will cause lseek( ) to begin at the end of the file, SEEK_CUR from the current file pointer location and SEEK_END from the end of the file. You cannot seek to a location before the beginning of the file though you can seek past the end of the file. If you seek beyond the end of the file, lseek( ) automatically enlarges the file. In any case, lseek( ) always returns the distance from the beginning of the file.

Figure 20-7 contains a program using random access file functions.

Figure 20-7. Use of Random Access File Techniques

```c
/* file4.c */
#include <stdio.h>
#include <conio.h>
#include <fcntl.h>
#include <io.h>
#include <stat.h>

main()
{
    int fd;
    int student_number;
    char ch,i;

    struct person_st
    {
        char name[80];                    /*Not a pointer!*/
        int test_score[10];
        int final_score;
    } student;

    fd = open("student.dat",O_CREAT | O_RDWR, S_IREAD| S_IWRITE);
            /* Open for reading and writing.  Create if it doesn't exist */

    if(fd)
    {
        do
        {
```

```c
    printf("Records for student #");
    scanf("%d",&student_number);

        /* Move file pointer to that student */
    if(lseek(fd,student_number * sizeof(student), SEEK_SET))

    {
        printf("\n(R)ead or (W)rite?\n");

    if((ch = getch()) == 'r' || ch == 'R')

            /* Read a student into the buffer and display it */
    if(read(fd, &student, sizeof(student)))

            {

            printf("Name %s\n",student.name);
            for(i=0;i<10;i++)
                printf("%d ",student.test_score[i]);
            printf("\nFinal score %d\n\n", student.final_score);

            }

    else if(ch == 'w' || ch == 'W')

            {

            /* Read a student form the keyboard and save it to the file */
            printf("Enter the name :");
            scanf("%s",&student.name);
            printf("\n");
            for(i=0;i<10;i++)

                {
```

140

```
            printf("Score number %d :",i);
            scanf("%d",&student.test_score[i]);
        }

        printf("\nFinal Score :");
        scanf("%d",&student.final_score);
        if(!write(fd,&student,sizeof(student)))
            printf("Write failed!\n");

    }

    }

    while (ch != 'q' && ch != 'Q');

    close(fd);

}
```

As you can see, even the simplest programs involving random access file functions can be somewhat complex. This program is quite powerful. It allows you to store a list of students and test scores. The length of this list is limited only by disk space. In addition, data placed in this list will still be available after the program exits.

There are a few important things to notice about this program. First of all, the structure being saved contains no pointers. It's imperative that you never save pointers to a disk file. Pointers are only valid when pointing at something in memory. There is no guarantee that a pointer will have identical values on consecutive executions of a program.

Second, the sizeof( ) function is used in nearly every file function call. By using the sizeof( ) function, you can pass the function the correct number of bytes to read or write without having to determine this number yourself.

Finally, it's important that you close all random access files. C automatically closes all file streams when the program exits. This isn't true of random access files. If they aren't closed when the program exits, such files will be truncated to a length of 0 bytes.

Random access file functions are both more complex and far more powerful than their sequential counterparts. By treating the file offset as a pointer, you can create almost any data structure on the disk that can be created in memory. While it doesn't make sense to store pointers in a disk file, it's perfectly acceptable to store file offsets there. This allows you to create pointerlike structures in a file.

Chapter 21
Printers and Other Devices

In *Turbo C*, the printer is accessed very much like a file. Data is written to it using the standard file commands. For obvious reasons, you cannot read from the printer. You can only write to it.

Turbo C does provide a standard printer stream called stdprn. You can use this stream with fprintf( ) to send information to the printer. The example below shows how this is done.

fprint(stdprn,"This will be sent to the printer \ n");

This assumes that a printer is connected and online. If this isn't the case, the effects of this function will vary depending on the type of machine. Some machines will simply send this data to a nonexistent printer. Others will wait for the printer to appear. There's a way to see if the printer is ready to receive data, but this involves the use of special interrupt functions. These will be described more fully in Chapter 24.

Unfortunately, the use of the stdprn stream isn't compatible with OS/2. If you're going to be running your programs using only MS-DOS or PC-DOS this won't be of any consequence. If you plan to use your programs with OS/2, you should avoid using this stream. Instead, you should create your own stream and direct it to the printer. This isn't as difficult as it sounds.

Creating Your Own Stream

As you saw in the previous chapter, CON can be used in place of a filename to refer to the screen. You can refer to any of the parallel and serial ports in a similar manner. For example, opening a stream using the filename COM1 would direct all data sent to that stream to the COM1 port.

Printers usually are connected to LPT1 so you can open your own printer stream with an fopen( ) function call as shown in Figure 21-1.

Figure 21-1. Opening a Printer Stream to LPT1

```
main()
{

int prn

prn = fopen("LPT1", "w");

fprintf(prn, "This will be sent to the printer\n");

}
```

Once the printer stream has been opened, it may be treated just like any other write-only stream.

Printer Commands

Printers are much more complicated than screens, however. Many printers will allow you to print in different fonts, sizes, and type styles. Many printers even offer graphic options. Accessing these can be difficult, however. This problem is compounded by the fact that the commands used to produce certain results can vary tremendously from printer to printer. This section will describe some of the basic ideas of embedded printer commands. For more details, please see your printer manual.

Most printers have a certain command character (usually the Esc character—character 27) that signals the beginning of a printer command. The next few characters then will be taken by the printer as commands and not as characters to be printed. The main difficulty in sending these characters is that they often aren't normal ASCII characters and thus cannot be easily placed in a string.

There are two methods for placing such characters in a string; neither of them is very pretty to look at. First, the more obvious way: A string is just an array of characters.

You can just assign the ASCII values of the special characters that you need to the appropriate array locations. Figure 21-2 provides an example of this using hypothetical printer commands.

Figure 21-2. Placing Non-ASCII Printer Commands in a String

```
main()
{

#define ESC 27

char bold_hello[20] = "000hello000"; /*Zeros will be replaced*/
bold_hello[0] = ESC;
bold_hello[1] = 6;        /*Change font*/
bold_hello[2] = 2;        /*Boldface*/
bold_hello[8] = ESC;
bold_hello[9] = 6;        /*Change font*/
bold_hello[10] = 1;       /*Normal type*/

fprintf(stdprn,bold_hello);

}
```

The second method employs a little-used feature of string functions. If you use a backslash and a three-digit octal number, the ASCII character corresponding to that number will be placed in the string. If you use x and any three-digit hexadecimal number, the ASCII character corresponding to that number will be placed in the string.

Unfortunately there is no way to place a decimal number in the string. You must convert the value to octal or hexadecimal before proceeding. The line below shows how this feature may be used to accomplish the same task as in Figure 21-2.

fprintf(stdprn,"\033\006\002 Hello\033\006\001");

Either method will do the job. It would be tempting to use macros to refer to these strings of control codes. This won't work, however, because the preprocessor doesn't replace any text inside strings. Consider Figure 21-3.

Figure 21-3. Trying to Use Macros to Embed Printer Commands

```
main()
{

#define BOLD \033\006\002
#define NORMAL \033\006\001

fprintf(stdprn,"BOLDhelloNORMAL");

}
```

This wouldn't produce the desired result. It would send the string *BOLDhelloNORMAL* to the printer, which would then appear on paper as shown.

The solution to this problem is a special feature of *Turbo C* called *automatic string concatenation*. Whenever *Turbo C* sees two strings separated by nothing but blanks, tabs, or carriage returns, it combines them into a single string. Thus

"\033\006\002""hello""\033\006\001"

is converted by the compiler to

"\033\006\002 hello\033\006\001"

Though the purpose of this is to allow strings to occupy several lines, you can use this method to embed printer commands within a string. While a string can't contain a macro, a macro can contain a string. Thus, you can use the macros defined in Figure 21-4.

Figure 21-4. Macros Containing Strings

```
main()
{

#define BOLD "\033\006\002"
#define NORMAL "\033\006\001"

fprintf(stdprn,BOLD"hello"NORMAL);

}
```

This method allows you to give names to control codes. You can insert macros inside a string using the same method as in Figure 21-5.

Figure 21-5. Inserting Macros Within a String

```
main()
{


#define BOLD "\033\006\002"
#define NORMAL "\033\006\001"

fprintf(stdprn,"The word is"BOLD"hello"NORMAL", ok?");


}
```

Warning: This is an extension of C and not a standard part of C. It only works using *Turbo C.* If you only intend to use *Turbo C,* by all means use this feature. If you intend to port your programs to other versions of C, especially C on some machine other than the PC, avoid using automatic string concatenation. By sticking to standard C conventions, you can keep conversion time to a minimum.

Peripherals That Aren't Printers

Devices other than printers can be used in a similar fashion. For example, a modem could be accessed from C by opening the port to which it's attached as a stream with both read and write capabilities. This might take the form

mod = fopen("COM1","rw");

Once this is done, printing to the stream mod will send data to the modem; reading from this stream will attempt to read data from the modem (possibly waiting for data to appear). As with printers, modems, as well as most other devices, must be sent special command strings to operate. See the device's manual for more details on its use.

As you can see, C treats all devices much the same as it treats the keyboard (also known as the console) and screen. The primary difference between the console and most other devices is that the console requires no special command characters.

Chapter 22

Memory Models:
Near and Far Pointers

Turbo C was built to take advantage of the 8088 series of microprocessors. Most IBM or IBM-compatible machines use either the 8088, 8086, 80286, or 80386. Normally C keeps the details of these microprocessors hidden from you.

Addressing Memory with the 8088 Family of Microprocessors

The 8088 series of microprocessors uses what is called *segmented memory management*. You might think of memory as a series of addresses beginning at 0 and going up to the highest address in the machine. With segmented memory, this is a gross oversimplification. The IBM uses two registers to reference a memory location. One register contains a number in the range 0–65535 (64K). This number is called the *memory offset*. A second register, also containing a number between 0 and 65535, holds an address of a *segment* divided by 16.

A segment is a 64K block of memory into which the offset always points. Thus, to determine an actual memory address, you must take the segment register, multiply it by 16 and add the offset.

The microprocessor keeps track of most of the math described above, so you may wonder why you need to worry about it at all. Perhaps the following discussion will explain.

Part of the purpose of a segmented architecture is the fact that program speed can be increased if all memory accesses are confined to a single 64K segment. If this is the case, the segment register never changes. Only the offset is changed. This limits the user to 64K, however.

The IBM PC actually contains four segment registers. The CS (Code Segment) register points to the segment that contains executable code. The DS (Data Segment) register points to the segment that contains data used by programs (such as global or static variables). The SS (Stack Segment) register points to the segment that holds more transitory objects such as local variables. Finally, the ES (Extended Segment) register is provided as a spare register not usually used in C.

Any data object can be accessed in one of two different ways: *near* or *far*. If it's accessed as a *near object,* its address is determined by taking an offset and adding the default data segment to it. All near objects must fit in a single segment. Thus, you're limited to 64K for near objects. If the object is accessed as a far object, its address is determined by taking a segment register value, placing it in the data segment register, and adding an offset. Thus your addressing power is limited only by the amount of memory in the machine.

The same theory holds for function calls. The address of a *near function* is its offset added to the default code segment. The address of a far function is its offset added to its own version of the code segment. Thus, while you're limited to 64K when using near functions, the amount of space used for far functions is limited to the amount of memory in the machine.

Memory Models

What memory model does C use? That depends on the memory model you choose. There six standard memory models:

Tiny
Small
Medium
Compact
Large
Huge

The default model is small. To change the model, use the -M option from the command line. The option -MS selects small model, -ML selects large model, and so on. You can choose the memory model option from the compiler menu under the options menu in the *Turbo C* environment.

The Small Model

When you compile a program using the small model, C makes all data objects (global and local variables) and all functions near. The stack and data segments automatically point to the same address. The sum of the space occupied by all functions must not exceed 64K. The sum of the space occupied by all global variables plus the space used by the stack for local variable storage as well as the space used by the heap to reserve space for malloc( ) also must not exceed 64K. Therefore, a small-model program could take up as much as 128K, with 64K for code and 64K for data.

Because only offsets are used, all pointers are near pointers. That is, they contain only offsets and use two bytes of memory space.

The Large Model

Large-model programs use far pointers for code and data. In addition, the Stack Segment register isn't necessarily the same as the Data Segment register. In this model, you can have many more functions in memory. Global variables have their own 64K segment. The stack can also occupy up to 64K. The heap, used by malloc( ), will occupy whatever memory is left unused.

Because both offsets and segments are used, all pointers are far pointers. These pointers contain both offsets and segments and occupy four bytes.

Medium and Compact Models

Most programs will use one of these two models. Small-model programs tend to be smaller and faster but are constrained as to the amount of memory they may use. Large-model programs can use any amount of memory, but tend to be larger and slower than their small-model counterparts.

Two hybrid models are provided also. The first of these is the medium model. This model is useful for large programs that use little data. This model is identical to the small model except that far pointers are used for all function calls.

Thus, while you're still limited to 64K for all data (global variables, stack space, and the heap), you aren't limited in the amount of code you can used.

The other hybrid model is the compact model. This model is useful for relatively small programs that use large amounts of data. It's identical to the large model except that near pointers are used for code; thus, while you aren't limited to the amount of data space, the program code may not exceed 64K.

A medium or compact program will run faster and occupy less space than its large counterpart. Both will run slower and occupy more space than their small counterpart.

Tiny and Huge Models

Finally, two specialized models are provided. A tiny-model program is similar to a small-model program except that the Data Segment and the Code Segment are always equal. Thus the combined total of all data and all code must not exceed 64K. This model is primarily intended for system utility programs in which size is a premium. The main advantage of such programs is that they may be converted into .COM files. A .COM file is loaded in a different manner from a .EXE file by DOS. It will load faster and occupy less space in memory.

The final model is the huge model. The huge model is identical to the large model except that the amount of global variable space can exceed 64K as long as no single variable exceeds 64K. Because most variables will be declared locally to some function, it's rare for the memory involved in global variables to exceed the amount provided for large models.

General Rules

Note that in any of these models, the size of code or data produced by any one file may not exceed 64K. You aren't likely to run afoul of this restriction if you break programs into separate files. A file would have to be on the order of 10,000 lines before it came close to this barrier. Beware of breaking files apart by using the #include directive. C still will consider them to be a single file.

It's possible to explicitly declare any function or variable
as near or far. This forces the compiler to treat a function or
data object in a certain way regardless of the model actually
being used. As you might expect, this is only done in very
specialized cases. You'll see an example in the next chapter.

Note that if you declare a function as near in a program
that uses far pointers to access functions, that function will
be accessible only from the file in which it resides. Note that
the static keyword has the same effect and will cause the use
of near pointers in all data models.

Even in a large-model program, no single data object
may occupy more than one segment. This is mainly a problem with very large arrays. When you perform any kind of
math with a far pointer, only the offset is used; the segment
is always left as it is. The address of an array points to the
segment and offset at which it starts in memory. To find an
element in the array, you must add the appropriate number
to the offset. Because the offset cannot exceed 64K, there is
no way to access any elements further than 64K from the beginning of the array.

A huge pointer is a special pointer that combines both
the offset and the segment in a single number. Because only
one value is used, it's possible to add numbers greater than
64K to it. This will allow you to create single variables that
span more than one 64K segment. Figure 22-1 contains a declaration of a very large array.

Figure 22-1. A Very Large Array Declaration

```
main()
{

int huge *arr1;

arr1 = malloc(50000);

}
```

In Figure 22-1, 50,000 bytes are reserved for the variable arr1. If arr1 weren't a huge pointer, you'd be unable to access anything beyond 64K. Note that in any case you may not create a fixed array larger than 64K. You must use malloc.

Here is a final rule for memory models. All object files that make up a given program must be compiled under the same memory model. Note that if you decide to change the model of a program, you must recompile all its associated files. Neither the *Turbo C* MAKE utility nor the project manager in the integrated environment will do this. You first must mark all C files as edited. You can do this either by editing all such files or by simply typing TOUCH *.C from the command line. TOUCH automatically marks a file as changed without actually changing it.

Memory models have three different aspects. Many programmers will never worry about them at all. Even the small model is sufficient to compile fairly powerful programs. You may find that *Turbo C*'s default model (small) is fine for anything you do. Some programmers may find their programs growing too large for small models. If this is the case, you should try compiling under different models until you find the one that fits. Only when you need to look at the internals of the IBM PC will you move to the third level. In this case, you'll use the near and far keywords and actually manipulate segment registers yourself. Although this is rarely necessary, the next chapter will describe some programs for which it is.

Chapter 23

Accessing Memory Directly

Normally *Turbo C* hides the mundane aspects of memory from you. While you know that every variable has a unique memory location associated with it, you don't have any way to use that information yet. So far, you can access memory locations by name only.

Many interesting areas in memory go unnamed. These include special memory locations used by DOS, other programs, or even devices such as the screen. By the time you're through reading this chapter, you'll know how to access all these areas.

Direct Memory

The concept behind direct memory usage is simple. A pointer variable simply contains a memory address. All you have to do is store the memory address you wish to use in a pointer variable and then use that pointer to access the memory location.

Figure 23-1 shows how you would print the contents of memory address 10.

Figure 23-1. Accessing a Single Memory Location

```
main()
{

int *look;
look = (int *)10; /* Assign look to point to memory location 10 */
printf("Location 10 contains %d\n",*look);

}
```

(Recall that the * operator turns a variable into a pointer.)

This seems simple enough. But wait, you've already fallen into the first trap. What model are you using? This is an important question. Consider the two major models, large and small.

If the program is compiled in the small model, all pointers consist of an offset only. The offset always points to a location in the data segment (unless the pointer points to a function). In the small model, the code in Figure 23-1 will examine only the contents of the tenth location in the data segment.

If the program is compiled in the large model, all pointers consist of both offsets and segment locations. Thus the pointer can point to any place in memory. In the large model, the code in Figure 23-1 will examine the contents of the tenth location in memory.

Far and Near Pointers

It isn't a good idea to have a program that behaves differently depending on the model used. It would be preferable to write a program that would examine the tenth address in memory regardless of model, if that were your desire. The way to accomplish this is to force the pointer used to examine memory to be a far pointer, having both an offset and segment. Figure 23-2 shows how this is done.

Figure 23-2. Using a Far Pointer

```
main()
{

int far *look;

look = (int far *)10;  /* Assign look to point to memory location 10 */
printf("Location 10 contains %d\n",*look);

}
```

(Note that the far keyword immediately precedes the pointer operator.)

The code in Figure 23-2 will always examine the tenth location in memory regardless of the model used. If you wish to constrain yourself to a single segment, then you can use the near keyword, as shown in figure 23-3.

Figure 23-3. Using a Near Pointer

```
main()
{

int near *look;
look = (int near *)10;
printf("Location 10 contains %d\n",*look);

}
```

To complicate matters further, no pointer is an actual physical address. In the case of near pointers, a pointer variable contains an offset in a default segment. This is clear enough. Far models are trickier.

A far pointer is always a segment/offset pair. It's important to remember this fact whenever you're using pointer arithmetic. Consider the hexadecimal address 0x12000. When assigned to a pointer, you might think it will give you the twelve thousandth (hexadecimal) memory location.

Wrong. Consider what happens when this value is assigned to a far pointer. The number 0x12000 is too large to fit in the single, two-byte offset, so the number 0x2000 is stored there. The remaining digits (0x1) then are stored in the segment portion (see Figure 23-4).

Figure 23-4. The Breakdown of Address 0x12000

Segment	Offset
0x1	0x2000

Now consider what this number means as a pointer. The segment is multiplied by 0x10 (16 decimal). This number is then added to the offset to determine that actual physical memory address (see Figure 23-5).

Figure 23-5. C's Interpretation of 0x12000 as an Absolute Address

Segment		Offset		Address
0x1		0x2000		
$1 \times 0x1 = 0x10$		0x2000		
0x10	+	0x2000	=	0x2010

Thus the pointer points to memory location 0x2010, and not 0x12000. Now you can see why hexadecimal numbers are usually used for pointers.

The math shown above would be a nightmare in decimal. You would have to divide the address by 65536; the result is the segment, and the remainder is the offset. Finally you'd have to multiply the segment by 16 and add that to the offset to find the physical address.

Great care must be taken that the correct segment and offset are used whenever constants are assigned to pointers. Fortunately, the most interesting memory locations are located in the first 64K of memory. Any number less than 0x10000 will reference a memory address in the first 64K of memory, as the segment register will become 0.

Uses for Direct Memory Addressing

So what's the use of all this? There are primarily two uses for accessing memory directly: to speed screen output and to access special areas of DOS. This chapter will cover screen output first.

The screen can best be thought of as a very large array of characters. Each character on the screen is represented by two characters in memory. The first stores the actual character, and the second stores its *attribute*. The attribute stores both the background and foreground colors of the character as well as values telling whether the value is flashing or bright. You'll read more about this later.

The screen is 80 characters wide and 25 characters high. This can be mimicked with an array declared as

char screen[25][80][2]

The first index represents the *y* (vertical) coordinate of the screen, and the second represents the *x* (horizontal) coordinate. The last index stores first the character and then the attribute of that location on the screen. Note that the indexes must be declared in this order to conform to the actual screen array in memory.

The memory address at which the screen starts varies with the type of equipment used. In text mode, it can be in one of two locations. In color systems, the screen will be at location B800:0000 (physical address 0xB8000). In monochrome systems, the screen will be at location B000:0000 (physical address 0xB0000). In order to create a variable that will treat this area of memory as an array, you must create a far pointer to the array described above. This is done in Figure 23-6.

Figure 23-6. Creating a Far Pointer to a Screen Array

```
main()
{

typedef char screen_t[25][80][2];
screen_t far *screen;

screen = (screen_t far *) 0xB8000000;

(*screen)[10][10][0] = 'a';


}
```

The first line creates a character array type that mimics the screen. All variables declared with this type will use the same format as the actual screen. The next line creates a pointer variable called screen that will be used to access the actual screen. Because the screen uses a segment of its own, this is a far pointer.

The third line assigns the location of the screen to the screen pointer variable. Note that the value used to reach the actual address 0xB8000 is 0xB8000000. Once this assignment is made, values can be sent to the screen using this pointer. The last line places the character *a* in the eleventh row and eleventh column of array 1 that our screen pointer variable points to. First, (*screen) dereferences the pointer variable — that is, *Turbo C* follows the pointer to what it's pointing to. As defined by the typedef, this is taken to be a 25 × 80 × 2 array of chars. Since this array is stored in screen memory, an *a* is stored at position 11,11 of the screen.

Figure 23-7 contains a more interesting program that deals with the screen. First the screen is cleared. Next, all attribute values in the screen are changed to magenta. Finally, each character on the screen is assigned a character corresponding to its row. If you run this program, you'll see just how fast direct screen writes can be. By writing directly to the screen, you're bypassing all those time-consuming text formatting routines used by printf( ). Of course, you're also losing all those useful text-formatting features.

Figure 23-7. Writing to the Screen with C

```c
/* clear.c */
#include <stdio.h>

typedef unsigned char screen_t[25][80][2];
screen_t far *screen;          /* A pointer to a screen */

main()
{
    int i,j;

    screen = (screen_t far *)0xb8000000;   /* Point the pointer to the color screen */

    printf("Press a key to erase the screen\n");
    getch();

    for(i=0;i<25;i++)
        for(j=0;j<80;j++)
            (*screen)[i][j][0] = ' ';      /* Set all screen characters to ' ' */

    getch();
    printf("Press any key to paint the screen magenta\n");
    getch();
```

161

```
                                                         /* Set all screen attributes to 0x50 */
for(i=0;i<25;i++)
    for(j=0;j<80;j++)
        (*screen)[i][j][1] = 0x50;

getch();
printf("Press any key for fun stuff!\n");
getch();
                                                         /* Set all screen characters to the row number */
for(i=0;i<25;i++)
    for(j=0;j<80;j++)
        (*screen)[i][j][0] = i;

getch();

}
```

Note that clear.c is meant to be run on a color system. If you have a monochrome monitor, substitute 0xB0000000 for 0xB8000000.

The attribute byte deserves more consideration. This byte tells the PC the color to make each character. The eight bits in each byte are broken down into four different sections as shown in Figure 23-8.

Figure 23-8. Altering Attribute Memory

These are the component bits of the attribute byte:

Flashing	Background	Intensity	Foreground
Bit 7	Bits	Bit 3	Bits
	6 5 4		2 1 0
	R G B*		R G B

Following are the colors that can be obtained by entering the listed three-bit values into the three-bit areas shown as RGB for foreground and background above.

Color	Decimal	Binary
		R G B
Black	0	0 0 0
Blue	1	0 0 1
Green	2	0 1 0
Cyan	3	0 1 1
Red	4	1 0 0
Magenta	5	1 0 1
Yellow	6	1 1 0
White	7	1 1 1

* R, G, and B stand for Red, Green, and Blue, respectively.

If the first (high) bit is set to 1, the corresponding character will be flashing. The next three bits determine the background color. Any of the colors shown in the latter half of Figure 23-8 can be used. The next bit determines the intensity (bright or dim) of the character shown on the text screen.

The foreground color is determined by the last (low) three bits. Foreground colors use the same notation as background colors.

Attribute Definitions

The easiest way to keep these attributes straight is to create definitions to refer to them. Figure 23-9 contains a header file with such a list of attributes.

Figure 23-9. Attribute Definition Header File COLORS.H

```
/* Colors.h*/


#define BRIGHT 8
#define FLASHING 128
#define BLACK 0
#define BLUE 1
#define GREEN 2
#define CYAN 3
#define RED 4
#define MAGENTA 5
#define YELLOW 6
#define WHITE 7
#define BACKGROUND * 16
#define FOREGROUND * 1
```

The macros BACKGROUND and FOREGROUND modify the colors to appear either in the background or the foreground (colors default to foreground, so this definition isn't completely necessary). To specify both a foreground and a background color, you can simply add the two corresponding definitions. You can also change the bright and flashing attributes in this way. For example, the expression

GREEN FOREGROUND + RED BACKGROUND + BRIGHT

would produce the correct attribute for a bright green character on a red background.

Figure 23-10 contains a function that will print a string to the screen at a specified location and in a specified color. The definitions created above are included as the file COLORS.H.

While the function print _ it( ) will work only with strings, it's fairly easy to build a string containing all of the appropriate values using sprintf( ). The program in Figure 23-10 does this. The print _ it( ) function gives you much of the power of printf( ) with some of the speed of direct memory access.

If you have *Turbo C* version 1.0, you'll find this function very useful. If you have *Turbo C* version 1.5 or later you'll notice that routines similar to the one above are available in the *Turbo C* graphics library. Because these library routines can use direct memory access, they're about as fast as routines can be.

This doesn't mean that the first half of this chapter was wasted. Using the concepts described above, you could do much that isn't available yet in a library. You could, for example, write routines to create the kind of pop-up menus that appear in the integrated environment.

Looking at Memory Directly

In order to describe the other interesting areas of the IBM PC, a program will be presented that will allow you to look at memory directly. There's no better way to learn about what the machine contains than to look for yourself. The program in Figure 23-11 will allow you to look at, and even modify, memory directly.

Figure 23-10. Function for Screen Printing print _ it( )

```c
/* Print_it.c */
#include <stdio.h>
#include "colors.h"

typedef unsigned char screen_t [25] [80] [2];
screen_t far *screen;

print_it(int x,int y,int attr,char *string)
{
        int i;

        for(i=0;i<strlen(string);i++)
        {
                (*screen)[y][x+i][0] = string[i];      /* Print a character */
                (*screen)[y][x+i][1] = attr;                /* Set its color */
        }
}

main()
{
        int i,j;
        char string[80];

        screen = (screen_t far *)0xb8000000;         /* Color screen */

        print_it(1,2,WHITE BACKGROUND + BLACK FOREGROUND,"This is a string");
```

```
        sprintf(string,"An int:%d and a float:%6.2f",12,34.5);

        print_it(1,3,BRIGHT + WHITE BACKGROUND + BLUE FOREGROUND,string);
}
```

Figure 23-11. Memory-Viewing Program scope.c

```
/* scope.c */
#include <stdio.h>

        /* values returned by getch() for some keypad keys */

#define UP_ARROW 0x48
#define DN_ARROW 0x50
#define PG_UP 0x49
#define PG_DN 0x51
#define HOME 0x47
#define END 0x4f

#define CHAR 1
#define INT 2

typedef unsigned char screen_t[25][80][2];
screen_t far *screen;

main()
{
        char huge *scope=(char huge *)0;            /* Start the scope at location 0 */
```

```c
long temp;
char ch;
char buffer[80];
int num, key;
int i,j;
int mode = CHAR;
int val;

screen = (screen_t far *)0xb8000000;    /* Set the color screen */

printf("Enter an address:");
scanf("%lx",&temp);

                   /* Convert to a far pointer */
temp = (temp % 0x10) + ((temp/0x10) * 0x10000);
printf("%lx\n",temp);

         /* Set the scope pointer */
scope = (char huge *)temp;
memset(buffer, ' ', 80);

while((key = getch()) != 'q' && key != 'q')
{
switch(key)
{
                       /* Perform the appropriate command */

    case UP_ARROW : scope -= mode; break;
    case DN_ARROW : scope += mode; break;
    case PG_UP : scope -= 0x10; break;
```

168

```c
case PG_DN : scope += 0x10; break;
case '-' : scope -= 0x100; break;
case '+' : scope += 0x100; break;
case HOME : scope -= 0x1000; break;
case END : scope += 0x1000; break;

case 'm' :    /* Change the display mode */
case 'M' : if (mode == CHAR)
                              mode = INT;
           else
                              mode = CHAR; break;

case 'e' :         /* Read a new address */
case 'E' : printf("Enter an address:");
           scanf("%lx",&temp);
           temp = (temp % 0x10) + ((temp/0x10) * 0x10000);
           scope = (char huge *)temp;
           break;

case 'v' :         /* change the current value that scope points to */
case 'V' : printf("Enter a hexadecimal value for address %p :",
                              (unsigned long)(scope));
           scanf("%x",&val);
           if (mode == CHAR)
                              *(scope) = val;
           else
                              *((unsigned int huge *)scope) = val;
           break;

case 's' :         /* Search for a word */
case 'S' : printf("Enter the search string :");
           scanf("%s",buffer);
```

169

```c
                                        /* Move through memory until a match is found or
                                                          until scope wraps to zero */
                        while(memcmp(scope++,buffer,strlen(buffer)) && scope)
        (*screen)[1][1][0] = (char)scope;
                        scope--;
                        break;

}

for(i=0;i<0x10;i++)    /* This loop prints the display*/
{

    if(mode == CHAR)
    {

        ch = *(char huge *)(scope + i); /* read as a character */
        sprintf(buffer,"%p:  %4o  %3u  %2x %c",
            (unsigned long)(scope+i),(unsigned char)ch,
            (unsigned char)ch,
            (unsigned char)ch,(ch==0 ? 32 : (unsigned char)ch));

for(j=0;j<strlen(buffer);j++)
            (*screen)[i+2][j+10][0] = buffer[j];

    }
    else
    {
```

```c
num = *(int huge *)(scope + (i*2));        /* read as an integer */
sprintf(buffer,"%p:%6o %5u %4x %1c%1c",
        (unsigned long)(scope+(i*2)),(unsigned int)num,
        (unsigned int)num,(unsigned int)num,
        (num==0 ? 32 : (unsigned char)num),
        ((num/0x100)==0 ? 32 : (unsigned char)(num/0x100)));

for(j=0;j<strlen(buffer);j++)
    (*screen)[i+2][j+10][0] = buffer[j];
}
}
}
}
```

This program uses the same concepts as do the previous two, though it's more complicated. Direct memory access is used in two places. First of all, the contents of memory always are displayed directly on the screen. This allows the program to update the display by overwriting older information directly, without scrolling.

Another variable, called scope, is used to look at the memory area of interest. Because this pointer will be used to look at any location in memory, it's declared as a huge pointer. If scope were declared as a far pointer, it would be restricted to a single 64K segment.

First, a value is read from the keyboard with scanf( ). This value then is converted to a pointer and placed in scope. Next, the program reads a key from the keyboard and uses a switch statement to perform an action. Finally, 20 bytes starting at the address stored in scope are displayed on the screen in a number of different formats. The program will continue to read keys and display memory until Q is pressed.

Each line in the display provides a number of different versions of the same value. First the address is displayed as a far pointer using the format command %p. A colon separates the segment and offset values. Next, the value of the byte located at that address is displayed, first in octal (base 8) notation, then in decimal notation, then in hexadecimal notation, and finally as an ASCII character.

If any of the keypad keys are pressed, the value of the variable scope will be modified, causing the program to scroll the screen display. Note how the keypad keys are defined at the top of the program. Unfortunately getch( ) doesn't work entirely correctly with the keypad. These keys are mapped over normal keypad characters. Thus getch( ) will return the same value for the letter *H* and the up arrow. In the next chapter, you'll see how to get a more appropriate mapping of keys to ASCII values using interrupt functions. The scope.c program avoids problematic keys. Because a keypad key uses *H,* this key isn't used as an actual command.

This program also responds to some other useful commands. For example, you can move directly to any memory location by pressing E. The program will prompt you for a new starting address as it did when first run. The display then will be updated, starting with the new address.

Pressing M will toggle between byte and word modes. When the program is in byte mode, a single byte is displayed per line of text. If the program is in word mode, two bytes are displayed on a single line. This is useful for looking at places in memory that use two-byte words extensively, such as the screen and the keyboard buffer.

Pressing *V* allows you to enter a new value for the top-most address in the display. Use this with care. As you'll soon see, some locations should never be changed.

Pressing S allows you to search through memory for a string of characters. You'll be prompted for a string (one word only). The program then will scan the contents of memory. If it finds the string, its address will be displayed. In order to let you know that a search is in progress, a character in the upper left corner of the screen is modified at each address as it's checked. You can use this feature to discover a number of interesting things about programs installed in memory. For example, search for the word *Copyright*. This will often find notices in memory-resident programs. For example, you'll find *Turbo C, Copyright Borland International* at the beginning of any programs compiled with *Turbo C*.

Pressing any other key besides Q will cause the display to be updated. As mentioned above, pressing Q will cause the program to terminate, returning you to DOS.

This program is important for two reasons. First, if you understand how this program works, then you'll be able to write a program that accesses any part of memory in the IBM PC. Second, this program will allow you to directly examine many interesting areas in memory. You'll probably want to compile and run this program in order to follow the rest of this chapter.

Memory Locations of Interest

The IBM PC family stores much of its key internal data in an area of memory located between 0040:0000 and 0050:0000 (actual addresses 0x400 to 0x500). Most compatibles conform to this; however, a computer need not use these locations to be considered 100-percent compatible.

First, some of the miscellaneous variables found in this area. The current video mode is contained in 44:0009 (one byte). These modes are listed in Figure 23-12.

Figure 23-12. Video Modes

Mode Number	Text or Graphics	Resolution and Available Colors
0	Text	40 Columns, monochrome
1	Text	40 Columns, 16 colors
2	Text	80 Columns, monochrome
3	Text	80 Columns, 16 colors
4	CGA Graphics	320 × 200 pixels, 4 colors
5	CGA Graphics	320 × 200 pixels, 4 shades of gray
6	CGA Graphics	640 × 200 pixels, 2 colors
7	Text	80 Columns, black-and-white
13	EGA Graphics	320 × 200 pixels, 16 colors
14	EGA Graphics	640 × 200 pixels, 16 colors
15	EGA Graphics	640 × 350 pixels, black-and-white
16	EGA Graphics	640 × 350 pixels, 64 colors

Memory location 44:000A (two bytes) contains the width of the page in characters. Memory location 44:000C (two bytes) contains the length of the screen in bytes. Memory location 44:000E (two bytes) contains the offset of the beginning of the screen. Note that the previous examples always assumed this to be 0, the first text screen. Eight screens are available.

Memory location 45:0000 (a 16-byte array) contains eight pairs of bytes holding cursor locations for each of the eight text screens. Memory location 46:0002 (one byte) holds the current screen being displayed on the monitor.

As you'd expect, most of these values shouldn't be modified. Reading their values can be quite useful, however. For example, all previous examples allowed you access to only one of the eight screens available in the default text mode. Using the above information, you could always ensure that anything written to memory was automatically sent to the correct screen. In addition, you could use the current screen display location to switch screens simply by storing the appropriate value in 46:0002.

Whenever you use these locations, be sure that you're treating the variable as a variable of the appropriate type. If it's a one-byte variable, access it as a pointer to a char, if it's a two-byte variable, access it as a pointer to an int. If you were to read a one-byte variable with a pointer to an int, you'd get two bytes — the intended byte and the byte that follows it. If you were to write a one-byte variable with a pointer to an int you'd overwrite the byte after it. To gain a clear understanding of these problems, use the M command with the scope program to switch between reading values as two-byte integers and one-byte characters.

Several other interesting things are located in this area between 0040:0000 and 0050:0000. For example, 46:000C contains the clock. This number is incremented every time a clock interrupt occurs (approximately 18.2 times per second). Whenever the current time is needed by a program, it can read this value and divide by 18.2 to obtain the number of seconds since midnight. Location 47:0000 is a special flag that is set when midnight is reached. This is used to increment the current date and to set the clock to 0.

You can use scope to see the clock in action. Move to address 46:000C and hold down the space bar. This will cause the display to be repeatedly updated until the space bar is released. You should see the value in this location change rapidly. Although this location can be used by your programs, there's an easier way to obtain the current time using a special interrupt function described in the next chapter.

Another useful area of memory is the keyboard buffer. Every time a key is pressed, it's placed in a special area of memory. Any functions that read characters from the keyboard take them from this buffer. To find this buffer, you must use the two integer variables at locations 41:000A and 41:000C. Location 41:000A contains the address of the oldest character in the buffer. This is the character that will be read next by any of the input functions. Location 41:000C contains the address of the most recently typed character.

Normally these two pointers will point to a location in the 32-byte area beginning at 41:000E. Each character is represented by two bytes. The first byte normally holds the ASCII value of the key pressed. The second byte holds the scan code of the character. These scan codes are merely a different way of representing each character. (Scan codes are given in Appendix D.) Non-ASCII keys, such as function keys or Alt key combinations, are stored in a different manner. The first byte will be 0 to denote a special character. The second byte then will hold the character ID (also shown in Appendix D).

Another interesting variable is the keyboard status codes in 41:0007. The two bytes located here are further broken down into 16 toggle switches, each of which stores information about the state of the keyboard. Figure 23-13 contains a list of the meanings of each of these 16 bits.

Figure 23-13. Individual Bits Comprising Memory Locations 41:0007 and 41:0008

Memory Location 41:0007

Bit   Meaning When Set

0   The right shift key is being pressed.
1   The left shift key is being pressed.
2   The Control key is being pressed.
3   The Alt key is being pressed.
4   The Scroll Lock is active.
5   The Num Lock is active.
6   The Caps Lock is active.
7   The insert state is on.

Memory Location 41:0008

Bit   Meaning When Set

3   The Hold state is active.
4   The Scroll Lock key is being pressed.
5   The Num Lock key is being pressed.
6   The Caps Lock key is being pressed.
7   The Insert key is being pressed.

Bits 0–2 are not used.

These memory locations allow you to determine the keyboard state without looking directly at the keyboard. For example, you could check to see if the Alt key is being pressed as is done in the program in Figure 23-14.

Chapter 23

Figure 23-14. A Program to Check Alt Key Status

```
/* alt.c */
#include <stdio.h>

main()
{
  int huge *status = (int huge *)0x417;   /* 0x417 contains
                                              the shift key status. */

  printf("Hit a key\n");
  getch();
  if (*status & 0x08)      /* Is the fourth bit set? */
    printf("Alt was used\n");
  else
    printf("Alt was not used\n");
}
```

To determine whether the Alt key is being pressed, the program takes the value out of *status (which has been set to point to the keyboard status variable) and strips out everything but the Alt bit by ANDing it with 0x8 (00001000 binary). If the fourth bit is set, the result will be positive. (ANDing with a value in this manner is called *masking*. The value 0x8 is called the *mask* because it separates out all unwanted bits of the variable.)

Note that you need not use getch( ). The getch( ) function is only used in this program to give you time to press (or not press) the Alt key. Otherwise the program would always see the Alt as pressed because the Alt-R command is used to run the program. This program operates on the assumption that no one could ever release the Alt key in the time between the getch( ) call and the memory access. Unlike using getch( ), reading the keyboard in this manner doesn't pause the program.

When the hold state is active (when Ctrl-Num Lock has been pressed) any program currently running is paused until a key is pressed. While this wouldn't normally be read (if the program is paused, it will have a hard time reading anything), it can be a handy way to pause a program without using getch( ). Note that this doesn't prevent interrupts from performing some action. It's quite reasonable for these routines (which will be described later) to read this bit.

Four of the bits control keyboard states. For example, in the Caps Lock state, all ASCII letters are capitalized automatically. In the Num Lock state, all keypad keys are treated as numbers rather than cursor control keys. Using the appropriate bits, you can read or modify these states at any time. Three of these states (Num Lock, Scroll Lock, and Caps Lock) correspond to lights on the standard keyboard. If the bit is set, the light is on; if it's cleared, the light is off. The program in Figure 23-15 uses this feature to selectively light the different lights.

Figure 23-15. Light Activating Program

```
/* lock.c */
#include <stdio.h>

main()
{
        int huge *status = (int huge *)0x417;   /* Keyboard status */
        char ch;
        int counter = 4;

        do
        {
                        /* Set one of the lock lights */
                *status = (*status & 0x8f) | (counter * 0x10);

                counter /= 2;                 /* Move to the next light */
                if(counter == 0)
                        counter = 4;
        }
        while((ch = getch()) != 'q' && ch != 'Q');
        *status = (*status & 0x8f);            /* Clear all lights */
}
```

Run this program and hold a key down. The lights will toggle on and off rapidly in succession. This is accomplished by selectively setting one of the three bits controlling the Caps Lock, Scroll Lock, and Num Lock states. First, the value located at 41:0007 is read, the three bits in question are cleared, and then the appropriate one is set. This value then is stored in the same location. This must be done in order to ensure that only the bits you want to change are affected.

Note that the IBM PC only checks the values of these registers when a key is pressed (any key, even a key that has no effect alone such as a Shift key). Thus the light won't light up immediately. It will wait for the next keypress. The program in Figure 23-15 uses getch( ) to ensure that a key will be pressed before each light is lit. If you were to remove these function calls, the program would attempt to light each of the lights in succession. None of the changes would be seen by the PC until a key was pressed. From the user's point of view, this would light a randomly chosen light whenever a key is hit. This isn't really a problem since these states have no real meaning until a key is pressed.

There are other more esoteric locations used by the IBM PC, but these are beyond the scope of this book. (You might want to take a look at *COMPUTE!'s Mapping the IBM PC and PCjr*, which provides an exhaustive list of standard memory locations.) Most only make sense when used by the operating system—for instance, the location that holds a value determining whether the machine is currently being rebooted. Any of these locations, including the ones described above, can be dangerous if not treated with care. The next chapter shows that much of the same information can be obtained through either BIOS or DOS calls.

Chapter 24

IBM BIOS and DOS Functions

In the previous chapter, you saw how to access many of the features of the IBM PC directly. Unfortunately, the memory areas discussed so far aren't guaranteed to exist on all machines, and sometimes they can cause problems when modified. The BIOS and DOS both provide ways of accessing these areas of memory through special function calls. These functions are much safer and will be compatible with any 100-percent IBM-compatible machine.

These functions are divided into two sets of functions: DOS and BIOS. The DOS functions are used primarily to access features of MS-DOS. They're considered part of the operating system. The BIOS functions are used primarily to access parts of the IBM hardware. They're considered part of the machine. This line is blurred by the fact that most DOS calls use BIOS calls to perform their tasks. Some BIOS calls are partially duplicated with DOS calls.

Both types of functions share calling conventions. These functions are called in a different manner from standard C functions. First, any parameters to the function are placed in machine registers. Next, an interrupt is generated, causing the function to be called. After the interrupt, any return values are stored in registers.

Calling these functions is fairly easy to accomplish in C. A number of keywords are provided for accessing the registers. For example, _AX refers to the AX register. These keywords can be used like any other register variables. Because they refer to registers used for other things by the system, they shouldn't be used to store data. The function geninterrupt( ) generates the interrupt. It takes one parameter: the interrupt number.

Every DOS or BIOS function call consists of three parts: the interrupt number, the function number, and the calling parameters. Every interrupt number can have a large number of functions associated with it. For example, most of the DOS calls use interrupt 0x21. In order for the interrupt to call the appropriate function, the function number must be placed in the AH register.

Because all such functions follow the same basic conventions, it's best to start with a simple one. Interrupt 0x21, function 0x2C will return the current time. It will place the time in four of the system registers (CH, CL, DH, and DL). Figure 24-1 contains a short program that will call this function.

First, the AH register is set to 0x2c. Then an interrupt 0x21 is generated, causing the appropriate values to be placed in the registers CH, CL, DH, and DL. These are stored in normal variables which then can be printed to the screen.

There are a few simple rules to follow when dealing with these functions. First, because the values in any of these registers is extremely volatile, you should always set them immediately prior to the function call and move the results to variables immediately after the function call. This is especially true of the AX register. *Turbo C* uses this register for all assignment operations. Thus its contents are scrambled by any such operation. Consider the code in Figure 24-2.

Figure 24-1. Calling Function 0x2C for the Time with time.c

```
/* time.c */
#include <stdio.h>
#include <dos.h>

main()
{
  int hr, min, sec, hsec;

  _AH = 0x2c;      /* The function number (Get the current time) */
  geninterrupt(0x21);      /* Call the function */
  hr = _CH;
  min = _CL;
  sec = _DH;
  hsec = _DL;
  printf("The Time is %d:%d:%d:%d\n",hr,min,sec,hsec);
}
```

Figure 24-2. Sending an Interrupt with Parameters

```
_AH = 0x2d;
_CH = 20;

geninterrupt(0x21);
```

The intent of this code is to call interrupt 0x21, function 0x2d. This won't work correctly as written. The first statement assigns 0x2d to AH. The next statement assigns 20 to CH. Because *Turbo C* uses AX (of which AH is a part) in all assignments, this will also store 20 in AX. At this point, AH will contain 0, the high portion of AX. Thus the geninterrupt( ) function call will actually cause function 0 to be called. Figure 24-3 contains a function where this is a potential problem. This function first reads the current time and then adds one hour to it.

Figure 24-3. Calculating Future Time and Risking Register Contention

```
/* time1.c */
#include <stdio.h>
#include <dos.h>

main()
{
        int hr, min, sec, hsec;

        _AH = 0x2c;                                /* The function number */

        geninterrupt(0x21);      /* Call the function */

        hr = _CH;
        min = _CL;
        sec = _DH;
        hsec = _DL;

        printf("The Time is %d:%d:%d:%d\n",hr,min,sec,hsec);

        hr++;
```

```
    _CH = hr;
    _CL = min;
    _DH = sec;
    _DL = hsec;
    _AH = 0x2d;                    /* Set the current time */

    geninterrupt(0x21);
}
```

In the second function call, it would be tempting to assign the function number to AH before setting the rest of the parameters. After all, it seems most natural to set the registers in alphabetical order. But, as you now know, this will cause the contents of AH to be scrambled before the function call is reached.

A final warning about register usage. You should be careful to preserve the contents of certain registers (CS, DS, SS, SP, and BP) as these registers point to important parts of the *Turbo C* system. In most cases, you won't need to change the values of any of these registers. However, some of the functions use the DS register as a parameter. Is this a problem? Will you have to save this value? Probably not. Consider the function in Figure 24-4.

Examine this program. It's supposed to create a directory named on the command line. However, it seems as though a parameter is missing. Where is the DS register set? Recall that all global data is stored in the data segment. Thus the DS register is automatically set to the segment that contains the global variable buffer. Note that if you tried to use argv[1] directly, or if buffer had been a global variable, this program would have failed in certain memory models. Parameters and local variables are placed in the stack segment, not in the data segment. To use a local variable in such a manner, you must temporarily set the DS register to the value of the SS register and then restore the original value once the function has been called. Figure 24-5 contains a version of mkd.c that uses a local variable instead.

Figure 24-4. Example Program mkd.c

```c
/* mkd.c */
#include <dos.h>

char *buffer[80];

main(int argc, char **argv)
{
    int result;

    strcpy(buffer, argv[1]);        /* Copy the first command line argument to          a buffer */

    _DX = (unsigned) buffer;        /* Set up the parameters */
    _AH = 0x39;                                      /* Function 0x39: Create subdirectory */

    geninterrupt(0x21);                  /* Call the interrupt */

    result = _AX;

    printf("The result was %d\n",result);
}
```

Figure 24-5. Using a Local Variable

```
/* mkd1.c */
#include <dos.h>

main(int argc, char **argv)
{
        char *buffer[80];
        int result;
        int oldds;

        strcpy(buffer, argv[1]);

        oldds = _DS;                    /* Save the old data segment */
        _DS = _SS;                      /* Get the stack segment */
        _DX = (unsigned) buffer;
        _AH = 0x39;

        geninterrupt(0x21);

        result = _AX;
        _DS = oldds;                    /* Restore the data segment */

        printf("The result was %d\n",result);
}
```

Note that both programs rely on the fact that the variables in question are located in the default segment. In large data models, this might not be the case for global variables located in different files. In such cases, the DS register may not reflect the segment where the variable is located. In these instances, determining the correct segment value can be very difficult. To do so, you must convert the pointer to a long and move the top two words to the DS register and the bottom two words to the DX register. It's usually simpler to copy the contents of the variable to a local variable and use that.

This function raises another interesting question. If you look at the function definition, it says that if the function fails to create a directory, the carry flag will be set. Unfortunately, the only way to determine if the carry flag is set is to resort to in-line assembly. Figure 24-6 shows an example of such a program. Because it contains in-line assembly, it must be compiled from the command line.

Figure 24-6. Testing the Carry Flag from Within a Program with In-Line Assembly

```
/* mkd2.c */
#include <dos.h>


main(int argc, char **argv)
{
        char *buffer[80];
        int result;
        int oldds;

        strcpy(buffer, argv[1]);

        oldds = _DS;
        _DS = _SS;
        _DX = (unsigned) buffer;
        _AH = 0x39;

        geninterrupt(0x21);

        asm jc fail             /* Did the function fail? */
        _DS = oldds;

        exit(0);                        /* Leave the program */

fail:
        result = _AX;
        _DS = oldds;

        printf("error! %d\n",result);
}
```

If you need to examine the carry flag, and you cannot use in-line assembly, there's a function that will call a DOS function and will return the carry flag. It's actually a Microsoft C function that was included in *Turbo C* for compatibility. Figure 24-7 contains a version of mkd that uses the function intdos( ). In order to use this function, you must set the registers in an entirely different manner.

Figure 24-7. Using intdos( ) to Read the Carry Flag

```
/* mkd3.c */
#include <dos.h>


main(int argc, char **argv)
{
        char *buffer[80];
        int result;
        int oldds;
        union REGS inregs,outregs;
        struct SREGS segregs;

        strcpy(buffer, argv[1]);

        #if 0                                          /* Instead of this */
        oldds = _DS;
        _DS = _SS;
        _DX = (unsigned) buffer;
        _AH = 0x39;

        geninterrupt(0x21);

        asm jc fail

        exit(0);

fail:
        result = _AX;
        _DS = oldds;

        #else                                  /* Microsoft does this : */

        inregs.x.dx = (unsigned) buffer;
        inregs.h.ah = 0x39;
        segregs.ds = _DS;

        intdosx(&inregs, &outregs, &segregs);

        if(outregs.x.cflag)                        /* Did it fail? */
        #endif
                printf("error! %d\n",result);
}
```

As you can see, the parameter-passing convention is completely different. First of all, registers are declared as parts of structures. The SREGS structure looks something like Figure 24-8.

Figure 24-8. Declaring the SREGS Structure for Figure 24-7

```
structure SREGS
{
  unsigned cs,ds,ss,es;
}
```

The REGS structure is declared as a union so that the areas of memory corresponding to each register could be accessed as either two-byte words or as single bytes (Figure 24-9).

Figure 24-9. Declaring REGS as a Union

```
main()
{

  union REGS
  {
    struct x
  {
    int ax,bx,cx,dx;
    }

    struct h
    {
      char ah,al,bh,bl,ch,cl,dh,dl;
    }
  }
}
```

Because they're declared as a union, the structures x and h actually point to the same area of memory. Thus assigning a value to h.ah will store a value in the same memory location as the high byte of x.ax.

You may want to use the Microsoft function call instead of using the *Turbo C* geninterrupt( ) call. However, the use of this function isn't quite as clear-cut as the *Turbo C* equivalent.

Selected DOS and BIOS Functions

There are far too many DOS and BIOS functions to describe them all in detail. The appendices contain brief descriptions of the major DOS and BIOS functions. The rest of this chapter will give an overview of the functions available.

Nearly all DOS functions use interrupt 0x21. These are the DOS general functions. They allow you to perform many high-level DOS commands, such as reading directories, and they provide many lower-level DOS functions, such as reading and writing data to the disk either by using filenames or by using absolute disk addresses. These DOS functions provide interface routines to read from the keyboard and write to the screen. They allow you to access special features such as the clock, and they allow you to perform some memory management.

Other DOS interrupts include 0x25 and 0x26 (absolute disk read and write) and 0x27 (terminate and stay resident). These interrupts should be avoided whenever possible. All three functions can be performed from interrupt 0x21. A final interrupt, 0x2F, controls the print queue.

The BIOS functions provide direct access to certain portions of the IBM PC. Interrupt 0x10 provides access to the IBM PC screen. This interrupt provides functions that read from and write to the screen, modify the graphics mode, control the cursor, and perform several other functions.

Interrupt 0x13 provides very low-level access to the disk. At this level, the PC doesn't know about any kind of file structure, so these routines are very dangerous. Interrupt 0x14 controls the serial port.

Interrupt 0x16 controls the keyboard. This interrupt can be used to read a key, determine if there is a key in the buffer to be read, or read the value in the keyboard status variable described in Chapter 23.

Interrupt 0x17 controls the printer. This interrupt can be used to write characters to the screen or to determine whether the printer is busy.

The appendices contain a more complete description of these functions. Few of these deviate from the calling conventions described in this chapter, however.

Chapter 25

The Clock Interrupt

In the previous chapter, you learned how to call interrupt functions already included in the system. The functions listed in that chapter aren't the only ones used by the PC. Others are used for special internal functions. For example, interrupt 0x8 is used by the system to update its clock (among other things). This interrupt is automatically called 18.2 times a second. You should never attempt to call this function.

So why mention this function if it shouldn't be called? Because you can attach your own routines to it. Then, each time the clock is updated, your routine will be called, regardless of what the machine is doing. This can be used to perform a number interesting tasks.

The first example will be extremely simple. It will count clock interrupts and print a running tally on the screen. Two functions are used to install interrupts. The setvect( ) function takes two parameters: an interrupt number and a function address. It then installs that function as an interrupt. Whenever that interrupt is generated, the function will be called. By contrast, the getvect( ) function takes an interrupt number as a parameter and returns the address of the function currently installed as that interrupt.

Most interrupts (such as the clock interrupt) have special system routines tied to them. These routines must be executed for the PC to run. If you install one of your functions over the original interrupt function, you must call the old one somewhere in your routine. To do this, you must first learn how to call functions by address. The first step is to create a function pointer. This is done in Figure 25-1.

Figure 25·1. Creating a Function Pointer

```
main()
{

typedef int func(void);

func *func_ptr;

}
```

The first of these statements creates a type called *func*. This type is a function that takes no parameters and returns an integer. The next statement creates a pointer to that type of function.

Interrupt functions are declared slightly differently from normal functions. They never return arguments. The word *interrupt* must follow the return type (which is type void). Interrupt functions may take parameters, but these parameters act slightly differently from standard parameters. Figure 25-2 shows a declaration of an interrupt function and points a function pointer to it.

Figure 25·2. Declaring an Interrupt Function and Pointing a Function Pointer to It

```
void main()
{

  void interrupt do_nothing()
  {
  }

  typedef void interrupt intfunc();

  intfunc *intfunc_ptr;


}
```

To call a function pointed to by an interrupt function, you must first dereference it (access the memory it points to) with *. You then use the normal function call syntax (see line below). Note the similarity to the screen access method described in Chapter 23.

(*intfunc_ptr)();

It's worth noting that this can be useful in applications other than interrupt routines, though this won't concern us at present. The information above is crucial to an interrupt handler. Any program that will use interrupts must take the following steps.

First, getvect( ) must be used to find the old interrupt handler. This address must be placed in a global interrupt function pointer.

Next, the address of your interrupt handler must be sent to setvect( ). This installs your routine.

Every time the interrupt routine is called, it should do two things. First, it must call the old interrupt handler to ensure proper operation of the operating system. Next, it should call enable( ). Whenever an interrupt is generated, the PC suspends all generation of further interrupts. You should reenable them as soon as possible. The function enable( ) will do this. It takes no parameters.

Finally, when the program no longer needs the interrupt routine, it should again use setvect( ) to reinstall the original interrupt handler. This should always be done before the program exits. If this isn't done, DOS will attempt to call the interrupt even though it's no longer in memory. This will eventually cause your computer to crash.

Figure 25-3 contains a very simple interrupt installed as the clock interrupt (interrupt 0x8).

Figure 25-3. Clock Interrupt count.c

```
/* count.c */
#include <stdio.h>
#include <dos.h>

typedef void interrupt intfunc();
intfunc *oldclock;

typedef unsigned char screen_t[25][80][2];
screen_t far *screen;

int cnt = 0;

void interrupt count()
{
        (*oldclock)();
        enable();

        cnt++;

        (*screen)[0][50][0] = (cnt/1000)+'0';
        (*screen)[0][51][0] = ((cnt/100)%10)+'0';
        (*screen)[0][52][0] = ((cnt/10)%10)+'0';
        (*screen)[0][53][0] = (cnt%10)+'0';
}


main()
{
        int i;

        screen = (unsigned char far *)0xb8000000;

        oldclock = (intfunc *)getvect(0x8);

        setvect(0x8, count);

        printf("Hit a key to start the countdown\n");
        getch();

        for(i=100;i>=0;i--)
                printf("The value of 'i' is %d, 'cnt is %d\n",i,cnt);

        setvect(0x8, oldclock);
}
```

The function count is the new interrupt routine. It first calls the old clock routine and then prints a running count to the top line of the screen. Note that none of the standard I/O functions are used to send data to the screen. Why is this?

Many of the DOS functions aren't reentrant. That is, they should never be called from inside themselves. Normally this isn't a problem, however, because they don't call themselves. If you use one of these calls inside of an interrupt, you could inadvertently call a routine that the program is already in. Suppose that a clock interrupt occurs while DOS has begun to process a function call. If the clock interrupt uses a DOS function, this will be called, effectively within the original DOS call.

Consider what happens when this occurs. Most DOS functions use a special buffer area for data. The first DOS function puts some data in this buffer and begins to operate upon it. This function is interrupted by a clock interrupt. This clock interrupt calls another DOS function. This DOS function uses the buffer, effectively destroying whatever is there. The DOS function then finishes successfully, passing control back to the interrupt handler. This interrupt handler then passes control back to the DOS function that it interrupted. At this point, the DOS function becomes completely confused because the data that it stored in the DOS buffers has been destroyed. The machine crashes.

If you run this program, you'll notice that both the count of clock ticks and the countdown in main( ) are displayed at the same time. Even though there are no explicit calls to the clock in main( ), interrupt 0x8 causes this routine to be called 18.2 times each second.

This is only the first step in interrupt function usage. In COUNT.C, you had to be sure to reset the interrupt vector back to its original value before leaving the interrupt. Had you not done this, the interrupt would have attempted to call the routine even though it was no longer in memory.

You may wonder whether this would happen if you left the program in memory. This is possible. You can leave the interrupt handler in memory and go to DOS. The keep( ) function (also known as *terminate and stay resident*) exits the program in a manner similar to exit( ). It doesn't remove the program from memory. This allows the interrupt handler to continue to run even after you've left the program.

The function keep( ) takes two parameters: The first is the exit status, and the second is the amount of memory to save, in *paragraphs*. A paragraph is a 16-byte block. Figure 25-4 contains a version of count.c that stays resident after you leave it. For now, 0x1000 paragraphs (64K) are reserved for use by the program.

Figure 25-4. A Terminate-and-Stay-Resident Program

```
/* count1.c */
#include <stdio.h>
#include <dos.h>

typedef void interrupt intfunc();
intfunc *oldclock;

typedef unsigned char screen_t[25][80][2];
screen_t far *screen;

int cnt = 0;                /* Start the count at zero.*/

void interrupt count()
{
        (*oldclock)();      /* Call the old interrupt */
        enable();

        cnt++;


        (*screen)[0][50][0] = (cnt/1000)+'0';
        (*screen)[0][51][0] = ((cnt/100)%10)+'0';
        (*screen)[0][52][0] = ((cnt/10)%10)+'0';
        (*screen)[0][53][0] = (cnt%10)+'0';
}


main()
{
        int i;
```

```
screen = (unsigned char far *)0xb8000000;        /* Color screen */

oldclock = (intfunc *)getvect(0x8);  /* Start the clock interrupt */

setvect(0x8, count);

printf("Hit a key to start the countdown\n");
getch();

for(i=100;i>=0;i--)
        printf("The value of 'i' is %d, 'cnt is %d\n",i,cnt);

keep(0,0x1000);        /*Keep 64k of memory */
}
```

Warning: Don't run this program in the integrated environment. (You can compile it there if you wish.) The integrated environment requires that any memory above it remain free when not running a program. You can install the interrupt handler and then run the integrated environment if you wish.

This program will act identically to the program in Figure 25-3 when it's run. When it finishes, however, the running count of clock ticks will remain. In fact, it will remain until you reboot the machine.

The 64K reserved for the previous program was just a guess at the amount of memory it would require. It would be more efficient to reserve the actual amount of memory needed for the program. This can be done after careful examination of the memory map in the *Turbo C* user's guide. In the small model (the default) the following facts are true: The CS register will point to the beginning of the code segment. The DS register will point to the beginning of the data segment. These registers are both segment registers and so hold a paragraph number (a memory address divided by 16). The SP (Stack Pointer) register contains an offset to the end of the stack. In the small model, this is also the end of the program. This offset points to an area inside the stack segment. In the small model, the stack segment is identical to the data segment.

To determine the size of the program, subtract the starting address (the CS register) from the beginning of the data segment (the DS register). This gives you the size of the program code. Next, add the size of the stack offset (SP) divided by 16 to convert to paragraphs. Next, 33 should be added. One paragraph of memory is needed to hold the fractional component lost in the division above. Thirty-two paragraphs are needed to hold special DOS buffers at the end of every program. The final formula is

(_DS − _CS) + (_SP / 16) + 33

Figure 25-5 shows a version of count.c that incorporates this change.

The next program will be much more interesting. It will use the clock interrupt to display faces on the IBM PC screen. Each time the clock interrupt is called, each of these faces will be moved one space. This will cause the faces to appear to bounce around the screen. Because it will be memory-resident, you'll be able to run any program on the PC as this face program runs.

In order to keep this program as small as possible, it will be converted to a .COM file. A .COM file doesn't require the 32-paragraph header section that a normal executable program does. Only tiny-model programs can be converted to .COM files, so this program should be compiled in the tiny model. The text of face.c appears in Figure 25-6. To run this program, compile it normally. Then type *EXE2BIN FACE.EXE FACE.COM* at the DOS prompt. This converts the program to a .COM file. Type *FACE* to run the program.

Figure 25-5. A Version of the Program with More Efficient Memory Use

```c
/* count2.c */
#include <stdio.h>
#include <dos.h>

typedef void interrupt intfunc();

intfunc *oldclock;

typedef unsigned char screen_t[25][80][2];
screen_t far *screen;

int cnt = 0;                    /* Start the count at zero */

void interrupt count()
{
        (*oldclock)();          /* Call the old clock interrupt */
        enable();

        cnt++;

        /* Print the current value of cnt */
        (*screen)[0][50][0] = (cnt/1000)+'0';
        (*screen)[0][51][0] = ((cnt/100)%10)+'0';
        (*screen)[0][52][0] = ((cnt/10)%10)+'0';
        (*screen)[0][53][0] = (cnt%10)+'0';
}
```

```c
main()
{
    int i;
    unsigned mem;

    mem = (_SS - _CS) + (_SP / 16L) + 33; /* Find space needed  for program */

    screen = (unsigned char far *)0xb8000000;        /* Color screen */

    oldclock = (intfunc *)getvect(0x8);              /* Start the clock interrupt */
    setvect(0x8, count);

    printf("Hit a key to start the count-down\n");
    getch();

    for(i=100;i>=0;i--)
        printf("The value of 'i' is %d, 'cnt is %d\n",i,cnt);

    keep(0,mem);                /* Reserve only needed memory */
}
```

Figure 25-6. A .COM Interrupt-Driven, Memory-Resident Program

```c
/* face.c */
#include <stdio.h>
#include <dos.h>
#include <conio.h>
```

```c
extern unsigned _heaplen = 500;
extern unsigned _stklen = 4000;

typedef void interrupt intfunc();
intfunc *clockint;

typedef unsigned char screen_t[25][80][2];
screen_t far *screen;

/* X,Y locations for each of 20 faces */
char x[20]={10,30,50,70,5,20,40,60,65,25,7,11,13,24,35,56,78,63,14,6};
char y[20]={5,10,15,20,2,5,9,22,16,13,3,4,5,7,5,6,7,2,4,5};

/* Depth of 20 faces.  In front of, behind or same level as letters*/
char z[20]={0,2,1,2,1,0,1,2,0,1,1,2,0,1,2,0,1,2,0,2};

/* X Direction of travel (1=right, -1=left) */
char dx[20]={1,1,1,1,1,1,1,1,1,1,1,1,1,1,1,1,1,1,1,1};

/* Y Direction of travel (1=up, -1=down) */
char dy[20]={1,1,1,1,1,1,1,1,1,1,1,1,1,1,1,1,1,1,1,1};

char color[20]={3,3,3,3,3,3,3,3,3,3,3,3,3,3,3,3,3,3,3,3};

/* This is the character and attribute that each face is sitting on
   top of. */
char oldchar[20]=
     {32,32,32,32,32,32,32,32,32,32,32,32,32,32,32,32,32,32,32,32};
char oldcolor[20]={1,1,1,1,1,1,1,1,1,1,1,1,1,1,1,1,1,1,1,1};

char clock_block=0;
unsigned counter=0;
```

205

```c
void interrupt showface(void);

void interrupt showface()
{
    register int i,ok,cnt;
    int newx,newy;

    (*clockint)();
    enable();

    counter++;
    if(!clock_block)
    {
        clock_block = 1;

        for(i=0;i<20;i++)
        if(!(counter%2==0 && i%2==0))    /* some faces moves only every other clock tick. */
        {
            cnt = 0;
            ok = 0;
            newx=x[i]+dx[i];                              /* move the face */
            newy=y[i]+dy[i];
            while(!ok)                                        /* Find a ok place to put the face */
                                                   /* If the current place is no good */
            {
                if(newx >= 80 || newx < 0)          /* Bad x location? */
                {
                    dx[i] *= -1;                       /* Bounce off edge */
                    newx=newx+2*dx[i];
                }
                if(newy >= 25 || newy < 0)          /* Bad y location? */
                {
```

206

```
            dy[i] *= -1;                                    /* Bounce off edge */
            newy=newy+2*dy[i];
        }
    if((*screen)[newy][newx][0]==' ')                       /* No letter in the way? */
    {
            if(z[i]==2)         z[i]=rand()%3;              /* Move to a new depth */
            else                z[i]=2;
    }
    else    if(z[i]==2)                                     /* At the same level as letters? */
            {
                z[i]=rand()%2;
                if(z[i]==1)
                    z[i]=2;
            }

    if((*screen)[newy][newx][0] == ' ' || z[i] != 2)
    else    ok = -1;                                        /* Letter in the way */
    switch(cnt)
    {
        case 0: dy[i] *= -1;                                /* 1st try, bounce */
                newy=newy+2*dy[i];
                break;
        case 1: dx[i] *= -1;                                /* 2nd try, bounce */
                newx=newx+2*dx[i];
                break;
        case 2: dy[i] *= -1;                                /* 3rd try, bounce */
                newy=newy+2*dy[i];
                break;
```

```c
            default:
                        newx = rand()%80;                      /* Last try, move to random spot */
                        newy = rand()%25;
                        cnt = 0;
                        break;
            }
            cnt++;
        }
        if((*screen)[y[i]][x[i]][0]==1 || (*screen)[y[i]][x[i]][0]==2)
                                    /* restore background for old face if it is there */
        {
            (*screen)[y[i]][x[i]][0]=oldchar[i];
            (*screen)[y[i]][x[i]][1]=oldcolor[i];
        }
        x[i]=newx;                  /* Save the new location */
        y[i]=newy;
        if((*screen)[y[i]][x[i]][0]==' ' || z[i] != 2)
        {
            /* Save the background for the new face */
            oldchar[i] = (*screen)[y[i]][x[i]][0];
            oldcolor[i] = (*screen)[y[i]][x[i]][1];

            /* Draw the face */
            (*screen)[y[i]][x[i]][1] =
                ((*screen)[y[i]][x[i]][1] & 0xf0) + color[i];
            (*screen)[y[i]][x[i]][0] = 1;
        }
```

```
                }
            clock_block=0;
        }
    }

main()
{
    unsigned mem = (_SP/16L) + 1;        /* Tiny model */

    screen = (int far *)0xb8000000;      /* Color screen */

    clockint=getvect(0x8);
    setvect(0x8,showface);               /* Start the clock itnerrupt */

    keep(0,mem);
}
```

Two external variables are declared. The variables
_heaplen and _stklen are special global variables used by
Turbo C to determine the length of the heap and the stack.
By default, the tiny-model heap and stack are made large
enough to fill out the program to 64K. Because this program
needs nowhere near this amount of space, the two length
variables are explicitly set to lower values. Note that unlike
most external variables, _heaplen and _stklen may be assigned values in their declarations.

Because the program is compiled in the tiny model, the
formula for determining the amount of memory is different.
In the tiny model, the code segment and the stack segment
point to the same location. Their difference is always 0. Also,
because the program will be converted into a .COM file, the
32 paragraphs for the DOS header no longer need to be added. The formula for a tiny model .COM file is

(_SP/16) + 1

A number of things happen during each interrupt call.
Each face is considered in turn. Some are considered only every other clock tick. This makes them appear to move more
slowly. The direction is used to find a new location. If something occupies this location, or if it's off the screen, a new direction of movement is generated. If no new direction can be
found, the face is placed at a random place on the screen.

If a face has a depth that is "behind" the screen (in the z
array), it's only actually drawn if the target location is a
space. If it has a depth that is "in front of" the screen, it replaces that letter. If it's at the same level as the screen, it
won't move into the same space as a letter (as described
above). If a face is drawn, the character it replaces is saved.
This allows the program to restore the character when the
face moves away from it on the next clock tick.

The function showface( ) is about as complicated as any
clock interrupt will get. When dealing with the clock interrupt, it's important to remember that a new interrupt is generated every 18.2 seconds. As clock interrupt handlers grow,
they begin to use significant amounts of time between clock
interrupts. This will cause system performance to decrease.

If, for example, a clock interrupt handler takes an average of 1/30 second to run, then out of every second, over half a second is spent in the interrupt handler (18.2 * 1/30). This means that the speed of any program run while a clock interrupt handler of this speed (1/30 second) is installed will be cut in half. If the clock interrupt takes more than 1/18.2 seconds to operate, then all operations grind to a halt. Your interrupt handler won't have time to complete its task before being interrupted by the next clock interrupt.

Note that quite a bit can be accomplished in 1/30 second. Even on the slowest PC, showface( ) should execute in less time than this. It's able to execute so quickly because it relies on direct memory writes to reach the screen, and it avoids all *Turbo C* library calls. The *Turbo C* library functions were built for power, not speed. Many of them will choke the average clock interrupt. The printf( ) function, for example, is too slow to be called from a clock interrupt unless special measures are taken.

Obviously one solution to this problem is to keep clock interrupts as fast as possible. Another solution is to execute the main body of your routine only every other clock tick, or every third clock tick, or some other multiple of clock ticks. Figure 25-7 shows a shell for such a routine.

Figure 25-7. A Shell for Occasional Clock Interrupts

```
void interrupt clock()
{
  static char cnt = 0;

  (*oldclock)();

  if (cnt++ > 18)
  {
    cnt = 0;
    /* main routine */
  }
}
```

The main body of this routine will be called only once every 18 clock ticks. This gives it approximately one second to complete before it runs into itself. Note that the old clock interrupt must be called during every clock tick (the time it takes to run is negligible, unless other extra clock interrupt handlers are also installed). Not only will this allow larger interrupt-handling routines, but it will keep interrupt handlers from hogging the machine.

For many applications, even calling a routine every 18 clock ticks would be excessive. When designing a clock interrupt, it's important to ask yourself exactly how often the routine must be called. The hardest part about creating a clock interrupt handler is preventing it from overrunning time limitations.

As it stands now, face.c isn't complete. For example, if you scroll the screen at all, the program quickly loses the locations of all previously drawn faces. There should also be a way of interacting with the program after it has been installed in memory. The next chapter will present two more interrupt handlers that will solve these problems.

Chapter 26
The Keyboard Interrupt

The keyboard interrupt is one of the most useful interrupts on the IBM PC. Any routine tied to interrupt 0x9 will be called whenever a key on the keyboard is either pressed or released. This interrupt is responsible for reading characters from the keyboard and placing them in the keyboard buffer. It also performs other tasks, such as checking for the Ctrl-Alt-Del combination and keeping the keyboard status variable up-to-date.

Using the Keyboard Interrupt

You can tie a routine to the keyboard interrupt in the same manner as the clock interrupt. Such a routine will be called every time a key is either pressed or released. Figure 26-1 contains just such a program.

Figure 26-1. Program nocap.c

```
/* nocap.c */
#include <stdio.h>
#include <dos.h>

typedef void interrupt intfunc();

intfunc *oldkey;

extern unsigned _heaplen = 500;
extern unsigned _stklen = 500;

        typedef struct shiftkey1
        {
                unsigned Rshift:1;
                unsigned Lshift:1;
                unsigned Ctrl:1;
                unsigned Alt:1;
                unsigned Scroll:1;
                unsigned Num:1;
                unsigned Caps:1;
                unsigned Insert:1;
        }shkey1_t;

shkey1_t huge *shift;
```

```
typedef unsigned char screen_t[25][80][2];
screen_t far *screen;

void interrupt Off()
{
        (*oldkey)();
        enable();

    shift->Caps = 0;              /* Turn the capslock status off */
}


main()
{
        int i;
        unsigned mem = (_SP/16L) + 1;         /* Tiny model */

        screen = (screen_t far *)0xb8000000;        /* Color screen */

        shift = (shkey1_t huge *)0x417;       /* Shift key status location */

        oldkey = (intfunc *)getvect(0x9);     /* Start the keyboard interrupt */
        setvect(0x9, Off);

        keep(0,mem);
}
```

This program disables the Caps Lock key. It does this by clearing the Caps Lock portion of the keyboard status variable after every keyboard interrupt. Note that this program avoids using a mask by casting the pointer to a special set of bitfields that correspond to the different bits in the keyboard status variable. This also enhances the readability of your program as you no longer need to refer to each of the bits by number.

Once you install this interrupt, the Caps Lock key will no longer work. When you press the keys, the Caps Lock light will turn on and then immediately turn off. The original keyboard interrupt sees that the Caps Lock light is on and sets the appropriate bit; then this routine immediately turns it off.

Hot Keys

While most keyboard-handling routines deal directly with the keyboard and characters read in through it, the keyboard interrupt can also be used to create *hot-key* programs. Such programs, once installed in memory, can be called up by pressing a certain key combination. This is a fairly easy task. To create a hot-key program, simply create a keyboard interrupt that looks at keypresses and calls the functions making up your program when it sees the correct key combination. Figure 26-2 shows a simple hot-key program. It prints a word to the screen when Ctrl-Alt is pressed. Colors.h is the header file created on page 164.

Figure 26-2. Hot-Key Program key.c

```
#include <stdio.h>
#include <dos.h>
#include "colors.h"

typedef void interrupt intfunc();

intfunc *oldkey;

extern unsigned _heaplen = 500;
extern unsigned _stklen = 500;

        typedef struct shiftkey1
        {
                unsigned Rshift:1;
                unsigned Lshift:1;
                unsigned Ctrl:1;
                unsigned Alt:1;
                unsigned Scroll:1;
                unsigned Num:1;
                unsigned Caps:1;
                unsigned Insert:1;
        }shkey1_t;

typedef unsigned char screen_t[25][80][2];
screen_t far *screen;
shkey1_t huge *shift;

print_it(int x,int y,int attr,char *string)
{
        int i;
```

```
        for(i=0;i<strlen(string);i++)
        {
                (*screen)[y][x+i][0] = string[i];
                (*screen)[y][x+i][1] = attr;
        }
}

void interrupt newkey()
{
        (*oldkey)();

        if(shift->Ctrl && shift->Alt)
                print_it(3,3,BLUE FOREGROUND,"Hello!");
}


main()
{
        unsigned mem = (_SP/16L) + 1;    /* Tiny model */

        screen = (screen_t far *)0xb8000000;

        shift = (shkey1_t huge *)0x417;
        oldkey = (intfunc *)getvect(0x9);

        setvect(0x9, newkey);
        keep(0,mem);
}
```

This program uses the keyboard status variable to read
the control key combinations. Programs can also look for key
combinations not stored in the keyboard status register.

Almost any program can be made to be called up by a
hot key. The only limitation is the amount of available memory on the computer. Because any hot-key program must
share memory with other programs, an effort should be
made to keep them as small as possible.

The next program is a modified version of face.c, first
presented in the previous chapter. This version will allow
you to change some features of the program while it's installed in memory. Figure 26-3 contains the new version of
this program.

Figure 26-3. New face Program

```c
/* face1.c */
#include <stdio.h>
#include <dos.h>
#include <conio.h>

extern unsigned _heaplen = 500;
extern unsigned _stklen = 4000;

typedef unsigned char screen_t[25][80][2];
typedef void interrupt intfunc();

typedef struct shiftkey1                    /* The keyboard status structure */
{
        unsigned Rshift:1;
        unsigned Lshift:1;
        unsigned Ctrl:1;
        unsigned Alt:1;
        unsigned Scroll:1;
        unsigned Num:1;
        unsigned Caps:1;
        unsigned Insert:1;

}shkey1_t;

shkey1_t huge *shift;
screen_t far *screen;

/* X,Y locations for each of 20 faces */
char x[20]={10,30,50,70,5,20,40,60,65,25,7,11,13,24,35,56,78,63,14,6};
char y[20]={5,10,15,20,2,5,9,22,16,13,3,4,5,7,5,6,7,2,4,5};
```

217

```c
/* Depth of 20 faces.  In front of, behind or same level as letters*/
char z[20]={0,2,1,2,1,0,1,2,0,1,1,2,0,1,2,0,1,2,0,2};

/* X Direction of travel (1=right, -1=left) */
char dx[20]={1,1,1,1,1,1,1,1,1,1,1,1,1,1,1,1,1,1,1,1};

/* Y Direction of travel (1=up, -1=down) */
char dy[20]={1,1,1,1,1,1,1,1,1,1,1,1,1,1,1,1,1,1,1,1};

char color[20]={3,3,3,3,3,3,3,3,3,3,3,3,3,3,3,3,3,3,3,3};

/* This is the character and attribute that each face is sitting on
     top of. */
char oldchar[20]=
    {32,32,32,32,32,32,32,32,32,32,32,32,32,32,32,32,32,32,32,32};
char oldcolor[20]={1,1,1,1,1,1,1,1,1,1,1,1,1,1,1,1,1,1,1,1};

char clock_block=0;
char onscreen=5;
char current_face=0;
unsigned counter=0;

intfunc *clockint;
    intfunc *keyint;

void interrupt showface(void);

void interrupt showface()
{
    register int i,ok,cnt;
    int newx,newy;
    int reg;
```

```
        (*clockint)();
        enable();
        counter++;
}

if(!clock_block)
{
        clock_block=-1;
        for(i=0;i<20;i++)
        if(!(counter%2==0 && i%2==0))
        {
                cnt = 0;
                ok = 0;
                newx=x[i]+dx[i];
                newy=y[i]+dy[i];
                while(!ok)
                {
                        if(newx >= 80 || newx < 0)
                        {
                                dx[i] *= -1;
                                newx=newx+2*dx[i];
                        }
                        if(newy >= 25 || newy < 0)
                        {
                                dy[i] *= -1;
                                newy=newy+2*dy[i];
                        }
                        if((*screen)[newy][newx][0]==' ')
                        {
                                if(z[i]==2)
                                        z[i]=rand()%3;
                                else
                                        z[i]=2;
```

```
        }
        else    if(z[i]==2)
                {
                        z[i]=rand()%2;
                        if(z[i]==1)
                                z[i]=2;
                }
        if((*screen)[newy][newx][0] == ' ' || z[i] != 2)
                ok = -1;
        else
        switch(cnt)
        {
newy=newy+2*dy[i];
        case 0: dy[i] *= -1;
                        break;
        case 1: dx[i] *= -1;
                        newx=newx+2*dx[i];
                        break;
        case 2: dy[i] *= -1;
                        newy=newy+2*dy[i];
                        break;
        default:
                        newx = rand()%80;
                        newy = rand()%25;
                        cnt = 0;
                        break;
        }
        cnt++;
}
if((*screen)[y[i]][x[i]][0]==1 || (*screen)[y[i]][x[i]][0]==2)
{
```

```c
            (*screen)[y[i]][x[i]][0]=oldchar[i];
            (*screen)[y[i]][x[i]][1]=oldcolor[i];
        }
        x[i]=newx;
        y[i]=newy;
        if((*screen)[y[i]][x[i]][0]==' ' || z[i] != 2)
        {
            if(i<=onscreen)
            {
                oldchar[i] = (*screen)[y[i]][x[i]][0];
                oldcolor[i] = (*screen)[y[i]][x[i]][1];

                if(i==current_face && shift->Num)
                                    /* Numlock on? */
                {
                                    /* Display as solid face */
                    (*screen)[y[i]][x[i]][1] =
                        ((*screen)[y[i]][x[i]][1] & 0xf0) + color[i];
                    (*screen)[y[i]][x[i]][0] = 2;
                }
                else
                {
                                    /* Display as open face */
                    (*screen)[y[i]][x[i]][1] =
                        ((*screen)[y[i]][x[i]][1] & 0xf0) + color[i];
                    (*screen)[y[i]][x[i]][0] = 1;
                }
            }
        }
    }
    clock_block=0;
}
```

```c
void interrupt keyboard()
{
    (*keyint)();

    enable();
    if(shift->Num)                          /* Is numlock on? */
    {
        if(shift->Lshift && shift->Rshift && shift->Alt && shift->Ctrl)
                                            /* All four keys pressed? */
        {
            int i;

            setvect(0x8,clockint);          /* restore the old interrupts */
            setvect(0x9,keyint);

            for(i=0;i<20;i++)               /* Erase all faces */
            if((*screen)[y[i]][x[i]][0]==1 || (*screen)[y[i]][x[i]][0]==2)
            {                               /* Erase all faces */
                (*screen)[y[i]][x[i]][0]=oldchar[i];
                (*screen)[y[i]][x[i]][1]=oldcolor[i];
            }
        }
        if(shift->Lshift)                   /* Left shift? */
        {
            onscreen++;                     /* Add a face */
            if(onscreen>=20)
                onscreen--;
        }
        if(shift->Rshift)                   /* Right shift? */
```

222

```c
                onscreen--;                               /* Remove a face */
                if(onscreen<-1)
                        onscreen++;
        }
        if(shift->Alt)                      /* Alt? */
        {
                color[current_face]++;      /* Change the current face's color */
                color[current_face]%16;
        }
        if(shift->Ctrl)         /* Control? */
        {
                current_face++;             /* Get the next face */
                current_face%=onscreen;
        }
}

main()
{
        unsigned mem = (_SP/16L) + 1;               /* Tiny model */

        shift = (shkey1_t huge *)0x417;     /* Cast the keyboard status as a
                                                                        bitfield */

        screen = (int far *)0xb8000000;     /* Color monitor */

        clockint=getvect(0x8);                      /* Start the clock interrupt */
        setvect(0x8,showface);
        keyint=getvect(0x9);                        /* Start the keyboard interrupt */
        setvect(0x9,keyboard);

        keep(0,mem);
}
```

223

In this program, the new keyboard interrupt handler first checks to see whether the Num Lock key is on. If it isn't, no further action is taken. If it is, the program then checks to see whether any of the Shift, Alt, or Ctrl keys is being pressed. Each of these keys causes a different action to take place. The left Shift key increases the number of faces. The right Shift key decreases the number of faces. The Alt key changes the color of the highlighted face. The Ctrl key highlights each face in turn. (The clock interrupt has been modified to display the current face as the solid face character rather than the open face character if the Num Lock key is on.) In addition, if the keyboard handler sees all four keys pressed at the same time, it immediately erases all faces and restores all interrupts to their original values, effectively disabling the program.

Many of the time constraints inherent in clock interrupts aren't as much of a problem with the keyboard interrupt. Even if a keyboard interrupt is generated before the routine handling the previous interrupt exits, there will eventually be breathing space when no interrupts are generated, allowing the older interrupts to complete. This isn't to say that speed isn't a consideration. If you tie an excessively large routine to the keyboard interrupt, you'll find that the IBM PC begins to respond sluggishly to keypresses. While a one-second delay may not seem like much, if one is inserted after every keypress (and every key release), typing becomes a nightmare.

These rules apply only if the original keyboard interrupt is called before your own code. Conceivably, you could perform some actions before this interrupt is called. In such cases, it's imperative that your routine is small enough to allow the original interrupt to be completed. If it's slow, a new keyboard interrupt could be generated before it completes, causing characters in the buffer to appear in the wrong order.

Improving face.c

This chapter will now leave the keyboard interrupt in order to correct a problem in face.c. As you know, the program becomes completely lost whenever the screen scrolls. It would be nice if the program could somehow detect that the screen was going to be scrolled and erase all faces, preventing them from being placed in a location unknown to the program. How can this be done?

As you saw in Chapter 24, interrupt 0x10 controls output to the screen. Most programs (including programs using the standard C libraries) use this interrupt to print to the screen. DOS uses this interrupt for all output. You could add a new interrupt handler to interrupt 0x10, one that erases all faces.

This interrupt is much harder to use than either the keyboard or the clock interrupt, as are all DOS and BIOS interrupts. As you know, interrupt 0x10 often requires parameters in registers. However, almost any C statement will change the values of these registers. Worse yet, when any C routine returns to the calling function, all registers are restored to their original values. This will remove any information that an interrupt handler was trying to pass back to the program in these registers.

In order to use these interrupts, you must ensure that the values in the registers immediately prior to the call to the original interrupt are identical to the values they contain when the interrupt is generated. In addition, you must ensure that C doesn't overwrite any values that are intended to be sent to the calling function.

Whenever a normal function is called, parameters are pushed on the stack. These parameters are then used by the routine and discarded when it exits. Whenever an interrupt function is called, the contents of all registers are pushed on the stack. When the function exits, the registers are restored to their original condition. The effect is that you can treat these saved registers as parameters. To facilitate this, *Turbo C* allows you to use any set of parameters in an interrupt function declaration. Note that unlike parameters in normal functions, these parameters don't change the way the function is called. They merely provide names for saved register values.

Figure 26-4 contains a modification of FACE.C that also traps the output interrupt.

Figure 26-4. face2.c

```c
/* face2.c */
#include <stdio.h>
#include <dos.h>
#include <conio.h>

extern unsigned _heaplen = 500;
extern unsigned _stklen = 4000;

typedef unsigned char screen_t[25] [80] [2];
typedef void interrupt intfunc();

typedef struct shiftkey1
{
        unsigned Rshift:1;
        unsigned Lshift:1;
        unsigned Ctrl:1;
        unsigned Alt:1;
        unsigned Scroll:1;
        unsigned Num:1;
        unsigned Caps:1;
        unsigned Insert:1;

}shkey1_t;

shkey1_t huge *shift;
screen_t far *screen;

/* X,Y locations for each of 20 faces */
```

```c
char x[20]={10,30,50,70,5,20,40,60,65,25,7,11,13,24,35,56,78,63,14,6};
char y[20]={5,10,15,20,2,5,9,22,16,13,3,4,5,7,5,6,7,2,4,5};

/* Depth of 20 faces.  In front of, behind or same level as letters*/
char z[20]={0,2,1,2,1,0,1,2,0,1,2,0,1,2,0,1,2,0,2};

/* X Direction of travel (1=right, -1=left) */
char dx[20]={1,1,1,1,1,1,1,1,1,1,1,1,1,1,1,1,1,1,1,1};

/* Y Direction of travel (1=up, -1=down) */
char dy[20]={1,1,1,1,1,1,1,1,1,1,1,1,1,1,1,1,1,1,1,1};

char color[20]={3,3,3,3,3,3,3,3,3,3,3,3,3,3,3,3,3,3,3,3};

/* This is the character and attribute that each face is sitting on
    top of. */
char oldchar[20]=
    {32,32,32,32,32,32,32,32,32,32,32,32,32,32,32,32,32,32,32,32};
char oldcolor[20]={1,1,1,1,1,1,1,1,1,1,1,1,1,1,1,1,1,1,1,1};

char clock_block=0;
char onscreen=5;
char current_face=0;
unsigned counter=0;

intfunc *clockint;
intfunc *screenint;
intfunc *keyint;
```

227

```
void interrupt showface(void);
void interrupt output(unsigned,unsigned,unsigned,unsigned,
                      unsigned,unsigned,unsigned,unsigned);

    /* interrupt 0x10 takes parameters! */
void interrupt output(unsigned bp,unsigned di,unsigned si,
                      unsigned ds,unsigned es,unsigned dx,
                      unsigned cx,unsigned bx,unsigned ax)

{
    int i,temp;
    clock_block = -1;    /* Don't allow the clock interrupt to change
                            the screen if anyone else is writing to it */

    /* Erase all faces before anything is put on the screen */
    for(i=0;i<20;i++)        /* Erase all faces */
    if((*screen)[y[i]][x[i]][0]==1 || (*screen)[y[i]][x[i]][0]==2)
    {
        (*screen)[y[i]][x[i]][0]=oldchar[i];
        (*screen)[y[i]][x[i]][1]=oldcolor[i];
    }

    _BX = bx;              /* Get all registers from saved register set */
    _CX = cx;
    _DX = dx;
    _AX = ax;
    (*screenint)();       /* Call old screen interrupt (possibly modifying
                             the contents of the screen */
```

```c
        ax = _AX;                              /* Restore all old registers */
        bx = _BX;
        cx = _CX;
        dx = _DX;
        clock_block = 0;
}

void interrupt showface()
{
        register int i,ok,cnt;
        int newx,newy;
        int reg;

        (*clockint)();
        enable();
        counter++;
        if(!clock_block)
        {
                clock_block=-1;
                for(i=0;i<20;i++)
                if(!(counter%2==0 && i%2==0))
                {
                        cnt = 0;
                        ok = 0;
                        newx=x[i]+dx[i];
                        newy=y[i]+dy[i];
                        while(!ok)
                        {
```

229

```
if(newx >= 80 || newx < 0)
{
        dx[i] *= -1;
        newx=newx+2*dx[i];
}
if(newy >= 25 || newy < 0)
{
        dy[i] *= -1;
        newy=newy+2*dy[i];
}
if((*screen)[newy][newx][0]==' ')
{
        if(z[i]==2)
                z[i]=rand()%3;
        else
                z[i]=2;
}
else
        if(z[i]==2)
        {
                z[i]=rand()%2;
                if(z[i]==1)
                        z[i]=2;
        }
if((*screen)[newy][newx][0] == ' ' || z[i] != 2)
        ok = -1;
else
switch(cnt)
{
```

```
                  newy=newy+2*dy[i];

        case 0: dy[i] *= -1;

                  break;

        case 1: dx[i] *= -1;
                  newx=newx+2*dx[i];
                  break;

        case 2: dy[i] *= -1;
                  newy=newy+2*dy[i];
                  break;

        default:

                  newx = rand()%80;
                  newy = rand()%25;
                  cnt = 0;

                  break;

    }
    cnt++;

}
if((*screen)[y[i]][x[i]][0]==1 || (*screen)[y[i]][x[i]][0]==2)
{

    (*screen)[y[i]][x[i]][0]=oldchar[i];
    (*screen)[y[i]][x[i]][1]=oldcolor[i];

}
x[i]=newx;
y[i]=newy;
if((*screen)[y[i]][x[i]][0]==' ' || z[i] != 2)
    if(i<=onscreen)
    {

        oldchar[i] = (*screen)[y[i]][x[i]][0];
        oldcolor[i] = (*screen)[y[i]][x[i]][1];
```

231

```
            if(i==current_face && shift->Num)
            {

                (*screen)[y[i]][x[i]][1] =
                    ((*screen)[y[i]][x[i]][1] & 0xf0) + color[i];
                (*screen)[y[i]][x[i]][0] = 2;

            }
            else
            {

                (*screen)[y[i]][x[i]][1] =
                    ((*screen)[y[i]][x[i]][1] & 0xf0) + color[i];
                (*screen)[y[i]][x[i]][0] = 1;

            }

        }

        clock_block=0;

    }

void interrupt keyboard()
{

    (*keyint)();

    enable();
    if(shift->Num)
    {

        if(shift->Lshift && shift->Rshift && shift->Alt && shift->Ctrl)
        {
```

```c
    int i;

    setvect(0x10,screenint);
    setvect(0x8,clockint);
    setvect(0x9,keyint);
    for(i=0;i<20;i++)                    /* Erase all faces */
        if((*screen)[y[i]][x[i]][0]==1 || (*screen)[y[i]][x[i]][0]==2)
        {
            (*screen)[y[i]][x[i]][0]=oldchar[i];
            (*screen)[y[i]][x[i]][1]=oldcolor[i];
        }
}
if(shift->Lshift)
{
    onscreen++;
    if(onscreen>=20)
        onscreen--;
}
if(shift->Rshift)
{
    onscreen--;
    if(onscreen<-1)
        onscreen++;
}
if(shift->Alt)
{
    color[current_face]++;
    color[current_face]%=16;
```

```c
		}
		if(shift->Ctrl)
		{
			current_face++;
			current_face%=onscreen;
		}

	}
}

main()
{
	unsigned mem = (_SP/16L) + 1;

	shift = (int huge *)0x417;
	screen = (int far *)0xb8000000;

	screenint=getvect(0x10);
	setvect(0x10,output);
	clockint=getvect(0x8);
	setvect(0x8,showface);
	keyint=getvect(0x9);
	setvect(0x9,keyboard);

	keep(0,mem);
}
```

Note the function declaration for output( ). Each of the saved registers is declared as an unsigned int. Take special note of the order in which they are declared. *Turbo C* doesn't check to see that the names you give each saved register match with the actual register it represents.

The new output interrupt erases all faces from the screen. Next, the saved registers in the parameter list are restored to the appropriate register (again, remember that any assignment uses the AX register). Only the AX, BX, CX, and DX registers are restored as only these are used as parameters to interrupt 0x10. Then the old interrupt is called. When it returns, the saved versions of the registers are modified to conform with the values in AX, DX, CX, and DX when the original version is returned. When your function exits, *Turbo C* will restore these new values to the registers. From the point of view of the calling function, interrupt 0x10 acts as it always did.

Now all faces will be erased whenever output is sent to the screen. Because new faces are drawn in at least every 1/18 second, their disappearance won't be noticed. If the screen is scrolled, however, the faces will be erased and thus won't scroll with the rest of the characters on the screen. This ensures that no faces will ever be lost by the program.

One warning: This won't work with programs that write directly to the screen. Because such programs bypass interrupt 0x10, your program has no way of knowing when they're writing to the screen. There is no easy solution to this dilemma. This is yet another reason not to write directly to the screen. Of course, you may have no choice. One solution to this problem is to save old copies of the screen and use memcmp( ) to see if it has changed. Not only is this slow, but it will only tell you that something has been written, not that something is about to be written.

Interrupt functions are especially valuable as debugging aids. Figure 26-5 contains a small memory-resident program that will display the contents of eight registers whenever Ctrl-Alt is pressed. Pressing Ctrl-Alt again will restore the screen to its original state. In order to accomplish this, the program should use the saved contents of the registers (the program should print the values of the registers before they've been modified by the interrupt function itself).

While this program is fairly simple, it could be used as the basis for a full-featured debugger. For example, you could combine this program with scope.c to edit memory while executing a program. You could also display the contents of the stack or the heap. You could even use the clock interrupt to create a constantly updated view of the register set.

Remember colors.h was the header file created on page 164. It is used in regs.c.

The last two chapters described the use of interrupt handlers to access the basic levels of the IBM PC. While installing interrupt handlers is a complex subject, once the proper methods are learned, you'll find that you can write them fairly quickly.

Figure 26-5. Program regs.c

```c
/* regs.c */
#include <stdio.h>
#include <dos.h>
#include "colors.h"

typedef void interrupt intfunc();

intfunc *oldkey;

extern unsigned _heaplen = 500;
extern unsigned _stklen = 1000;

typedef struct shiftkey1
{
    unsigned Rshift:1;
    unsigned Lshift:1;
    unsigned Ctrl:1;
    unsigned Alt:1;
    unsigned Scroll:1;
    unsigned Num:1;
    unsigned Caps:1;
    unsigned Insert:1;

}shkey1_t;

shkey1_t huge *shift;

typedef unsigned char screen_t [25] [80] [2];
```

237

```c
screen_t far *screen;

char background[6] [25] [2];                    /* Place to save the background screen */
int on_screen = 0;

print_it(int x,int y,int attr,char *string)
{
        int i;

        for(i=0;i<strlen(string);i++)
        {
                (*screen) [y] [x+i] [0] = string[i];
                (*screen) [y] [x+i] [1] = attr;
        }
}

void remove_win()
{
        int i,j;

        for(i=10;i<16;i++)                      /* Restore the saved background to the screen */
                for(j=10;j<35;j++)
                {
                        (*screen) [i] [j] [0] = background[i-10] [j-10] [0];
                        (*screen) [i] [j] [1] = background[i-10] [j-10] [1];
                }

        on_screen = 0;
}
```

```c
void display_win()
{
    int i,j;

    for(i=10;i<16;i++)                     /* Save the background to a buffer */

        for(j=10;j<35;j++)                           /* And clear the window */
        {
            background[i-10][j-10][0] = (*screen)[i][j][0];
            background[i-10][j-10][1] = (*screen)[i][j][1];
            (*screen)[i][j][0] = ' ';
            (*screen)[i][j][1] = WHITE FOREGROUND + BLUE BACKGROUND;
        }

    on_screen = 1;
}

print_reg(int x,int y,unsigned reg)
{
                    /* Print a four digit hex number at an X,Y location */

    int tmp;

    if(reg > 0x1000)
        (*screen)[y][x][0] =
            (tmp = reg/0x1000) > 9 ? tmp + 'A' - 10 : tmp + '0';
    if(reg > 0x100)
        (*screen)[y][x+1][0] =
            (tmp = (reg/0x100) % 0x10) > 9 ? tmp + 'A' - 10 : tmp + '0';
```

```c
            if(reg > 0x10)
                (*screen)[y][x+2][0] =
                    (tmp = (reg/0x10) % 0x10) > 9 ? tmp + 'A' - 10 : tmp + '0';
            (*screen)[y][x+3][0] =
                (tmp = reg%0x10) > 9 ? tmp + 'A' - 10 : tmp + '0';
        }

void interrupt show_regs(unsigned bp,unsigned di,unsigned si,
                         unsigned ds,unsigned es,unsigned dx,
                         unsigned cx,unsigned bx,unsigned ax)

    /* Use parameters to access the saved register set */

    char buffer[80];

    (*oldkey)();
    enable();

    if(shift->Alt && shift->Ctrl)      /* Ctrl and Alt pressed? */
    {
        if(!on_screen)  /* Is the window on the screen */
        {
            /* Display the values of the saved registers */

            display_win();
            print_it(11,11,WHITE FOREGROUND + BLUE BACKGROUND,
                     "ax = 0000, bx = 0000");

            print_reg(16,11,ax);
            print_reg(27,11,bx);
```

```
                print_it(11,12,WHITE FOREGROUND + BLUE BACKGROUND,
                         "cx = 0000, dx = 0000");
                print_reg(16,12,cx);
                print_reg(27,12,dx);
                print_it(11,13,WHITE FOREGROUND + BLUE BACKGROUND,
                         "ds = 0000, es = 0000");
                print_reg(16,13,ds);
                print_reg(27,13,es);
                print_it(11,14,WHITE FOREGROUND + BLUE BACKGROUND,
                         "si = 0000, di = 0000");
                print_reg(16,14,si);
                print_reg(27,14,di);
        }
        else            /* Window already there */
                remove_win();
}

main()
{
        int i;
        unsigned mem = (_SP/16L) + 1;   /* Tiny model */

        screen = (screen_t far *)0xb8000000;    /* Color Screen */

        shift = (shkey1_t huge *)0x417; /* Keyboard status register */

        oldkey = (intfunc *)getvect(0x9);       /* Start keyboard interrupt */
        setvect(0x9, show_regs);

        keep(0,mem);
}
```

Chapter 27

Graphics

The recent release of *Turbo C* 1.5 introduced a complete library of graphics functions. These functions can be used to create fast and professional-looking graphics with little effort. While they're called much like standard functions, they're actually contained in a separate library file. This chapter will describe the use of some of these functions.

Graphics Mode

Any object file that uses *Turbo C* graphics functions must be linked with the file graphics.lib. This can be done from the integrated environment by adding this filename to the project file or by typing *TCC PROG.C GRAPHICS.LIB* from the DOS command line prompt.

The IBM PC operates in two different modes. In text mode, only characters can be sent to the screen. No other graphics of any type may be used. In graphics mode, anything at all may be drawn on the screen. You may draw shapes of many different kinds and also write text using special *Turbo C* graphics library functions.

Using graphics in *Turbo C* is a four-step process. First, you must determine what kind of graphics hardware is available to the system. Once your program determines what type of graphics card is available, it must pick the correct graphics mode. There are actually a great number of graphics modes available. The choice your program makes will depend both on the hardware available and the resolution and number of colors that it needs to use.

Once your program has determined the graphics mode, your program will use another *Turbo C* function to initialize the graphics system in this mode. Once the graphics mode is initialized, you may use any of the *Turbo C* graphics functions. When you have finished using graphics, you'll use a final graphics function to return the screen to text mode.

Figure 27-1 contains a program that uses a number of graphics functions.

Figure 27·1. Graphics Program graph.c

```
#include <graphics.h>
#include <stdio.h>
#include <conio.h>
#include <process.h>

      int g_driver, g_mode, g_error;
      int MAX_X,MAX_Y,MIN_X,MIN_Y;

start_graph()
{
      char temp[80];

      detectgraph(&g_driver, &g_mode);

      if(g_driver < 0)
      {
            printf("No graphics hardware detected!\n");
            exit(1);
      }

      if(g_mode == CGAHI) g_mode = CGAC2;
      initgraph(&g_driver,&g_mode,"");
      g_error = graphresult();

      if(g_error < 0)
      {
            printf("Initgraph error: %s.\n",grapherrormsg(g_error));
            exit(1);
      }
      sprintf(temp,"the mode is %d",g_mode);
      setcolor(3);
      settextstyle(DEFAULT_FONT,HORIZ_DIR,1);
      outtextxy(40,1,temp);
      settextstyle(TRIPLEX_FONT,HORIZ_DIR,1);
      outtextxy(40,20,"Triplex Font");
      settextstyle(SMALL_FONT,HORIZ_DIR,1);
      outtextxy(40,40,"Small Font");
      settextstyle(SANS_SERIF_FONT,HORIZ_DIR,1);
      outtextxy(40,60," Sans Serif Font");
      settextstyle(GOTHIC_FONT,HORIZ_DIR,1);
      outtextxy(40,80,"Gothic Font");
```

```
        getch();
        rectangle(45,25,getmaxx()-15,getmaxy()-15);
        setviewport(50,30,getmaxx()-20,getmaxy()-20,-1);
        MIN_X = 1;
        MIN_Y = 1;
        MAX_X = getmaxx() - 70;
        MAX_Y = getmaxy() - 50;
}

main()
{
  unsigned int i,j;
  int x1=30,y1=90,x2=60,y2=21;
  int oldx1[100],oldx2[100],oldy1[100],oldy2[100];
  int dx1=5,dy1=7,dx2=3,dy2=6;
  int bx1=200,by1=145,bx2=200,by2=100;
  int boldx1[100],boldx2[100],boldy1[100],boldy2[100];
  int bdx1=7,bdy1=5,bdx2=4,bdy2=6;
  int time;

  printf("Run for how long? ");
  scanf("%d",&time);
  for(i=0;i<=49;i++)
  {
        oldx1[i] = 1;
        oldx2[i] = 1;
        oldy1[i] = 1;
        oldy2[i] = 1;
        boldx1[i] = 1;
        boldx2[i] = 1;
        boldy1[i] = 1;
        boldy2[i] = 1;
  }
  start_graph();

  for(i=1;i<=time;i++)
  {
    setcolor(0);
    line(oldx1[49],oldy1[49],oldx2[49],oldy2[49]);
    line(boldx1[9],boldy1[9],boldx2[9],boldy2[9]);
    setcolor(1);
    line(x1,y1,x2,y2);
    setcolor(2);
    line(bx1,by1,bx2,by2);
    if(x1+dx1 >=MAX_X || x1+dx1 <= MIN_X)
      dx1 *= -1;
```

245

```
if(x2+dx2 >=MAX_X || x2+dx2 <= MIN_X)
  dx2 *= -1;
if(y1+dy1 >=MAX_Y || y1+dy1 <= MIN_Y)
  dy1 *= -1;
if(y2+dy2 >=MAX_Y || y2+dy2 <= MIN_Y)
  dy2 *= -1;
if(bx1+bdx1 >=MAX_X || bx1+bdx1 <= MIN_X)
  bdx1 *= -1;
if(bx2+bdx2 >=MAX_X || bx2+bdx2 <= MIN_X)
  bdx2 *= -1;
if(by1+bdy1 >=MAX_Y || by1+bdy1 <= MIN_Y)
  bdy1 *= -1;
if(by2+bdy2 >=MAX_Y || by2+bdy2 <= MIN_Y)
  bdy2 *= -1;
for(j=49;j>0;j--)
{
          oldx1[j] = oldx1[j-1];
          oldy1[j] = oldy1[j-1];
          oldx2[j] = oldx2[j-1];
          oldy2[j] = oldy2[j-1];
          if(j<=10)
          {
                  boldx1[j] = boldx1[j-1];
                  boldy1[j] = boldy1[j-1];
                  boldx2[j] = boldx2[j-1];
                  boldy2[j] = boldy2[j-1];
          }
}
oldx1[0] = x1;
oldx2[0] = x2;
oldy1[0] = y1;
oldy2[0] = y2;
x1 += dx1;
x2 += dx2;
y1 += dy1;
y2 += dy2;
boldx1[0] = bx1;
boldx2[0] = bx2;
boldy1[0] = by1;
boldy2[0] = by2;
bx1 += bdx1;
bx2 += bdx2;
by1 += bdy1;
by2 += bdy2;
}
closegraph();
}
```

246

Two global integer variables are necessary when using the *Turbo C* graphics functions. The g_driver variable will contain a number that represents the graphics card available on your system. The variable g_mode will contain the graphics mode that will be used by your program.

In any program that uses graphics, you'll start by calling the function detectgraph( ). This function takes two pointers to integers as parameters. These parameters are the two global integers mentioned above. The function detectgraph( ) will use these pointers to return the type of graphics adapter available as well as a graphics mode.

When detectgraph( ) returns, g_driver will contain a number representing the type of graphics hardware installed. A list of these numbers appears in Figure 27-2. Macros have been defined for each of these drivers so you need not remember the numbers. These macros appear in the header file graphics.h.

Figure 27-2. Common Values for g_driver

Value	Meaning
0	Autodetect
1	CGA
2	MCGA
3	EGA
9	VGA

The variable g_mode will contain the best graphics mode available for the hardware indicated by g_driver. *Turbo C* defines *best mode* as the mode with the highest resolution. If you have CGA graphics, for example, *Turbo C* will consider 640 × 200 monochrome graphics better than 320 × 200 color graphics. If you object to the choice of mode made by detectgraph( ), it may be changed simply by changing g_mode before graphics are initialized. A list of possible modes (macros have also been defined for these in graphics.h) appears in Figure 27-3.

Figure 27-3. Common Values for g_mode

g_driver	g_mode	Resolution
1 (CGA)	0–3*	320 × 200
	4	640 × 200
2 (MCGA)	0–3*	320 × 200
	4	640 × 200
	5	640 × 480
3 (EGA)	0	640 × 200
	1	640 × 350
9 (VGA)	0	640 × 200
	1	640 × 350
	2	640 × 480

* Values 0–3 refer to palettes 0–3.

Once the graphics hardware and mode are determined, you can initialize the graphics system. This is done with initgraph( ). This function takes three parameters. The first two are identical to the parameters for detectgraph( ). The variable g_driver must contain the number representing the installed graphics card. The variable g_mode must contain the number representing the desired graphics mode. These can be assigned either by the programmer or with detectgraph( ). The final parameter is a character string that tells *Turbo C* where the graphics drivers are located. In most cases, you'll simply use a null string (" ") to signify the current working directory.

Graphics and Text

The graphics text functions are quite powerful, allowing text justification and different fonts. The function outtextxy( ) has three parameters. The first two describe an *x,y* coordinate on the screen. The third parameter contains a character string. Outtextxy( ) will print this text string at the *x,y* coordinates in the first two parameters.

In order to center text, your program should use the function getmaxx( ). This function will return the *x* coordinate of the right edge of the screen. By dividing this by 2, you can obtain the coordinate of the middle of the screen. Note that this function may return different values for different graphics modes. By using getmaxx( ) rather than assuming some value of *x*, the program ensures that the string will appear in the middle of the screen regardless of the hardware.

Outtextxy( ) always uses the current text color, style, and justification. Functions are used to change the current color, style, and justification. Setcolor( ) takes one parameter: an integer that stands for a color. The number of colors as well as the color assigned to each number varies with the graphics mode. The function settextjustfy takes two parameters: the horizontal justification and the vertical justification. Possible values for these settings are shown in Figure 27-4.

Figure 27-4. Values Passed to settextjustify

Value   Justification

Horizontal

0	Left
1	Center
2	Right

Vertical

0	Bottom
1	Center
2	Top

Settextstyle( ) has three parameters — the font, the direction, and the character size. The basic fonts are listed in Figure 27-5 and are defined as macros in graphics.h. Two directions may be chosen. HORIZ_DIR causes all text to be printed horizontally from left to right. VERT_DIR causes all text to be printed vertically from bottom to top.

Figure 27-5. Fonts

Value	Font
0	Default
1	Triplex
2	Small
3	Sans Serif
4	Gothic

Line Graphics and Viewports

Turbo C provides a number of functions that draw shapes on the IBM PC graphics screen. The program in Figure 27-1 uses some of these functions. Most of these functions will draw in the current pen color.

The line( ) function is used to draw lines on the screen. Line( ) takes four parameters. These hold the *x* and *y* coordinates of the two endpoints of the line.

The rectangle( ) function draws a rectangle on the screen. Rectangle( ) takes four parameters. The first two parameters indicate the *x,y* coordinates of the upper left corner of the rectangle, and the last two parameters indicate the *x,y* coordinates of the lower right corner of the rectangle.

Setviewport( ) is used by the program in Figure 27-1 to restrict all output to the area inside the rectangle. The first four parameters specify the rectangle in which to draw all graphics. The fifth parameter is called the *clipping flag*. If this flag is TRUE, no graphics will be printed outside of the rectangle. If, for instance, you draw a line that extends out of the rectangle and this flag is TRUE, only the portion of the line that falls within the rectangle will be drawn. This process is known as *clipping*. If the clipping flag is FALSE, no clipping is done and some graphics may be printed outside of the rectangle.

To return to the text screen, you must use the closegraph( ) function. This function has no parameters.

Compatibility

Unfortunately, none of the *Turbo C* graphics functions are
compatible with any other version of C. Any program written to use them will have to be modified in order to run under different versions of C.

There are no clear-cut graphics standards, so there is no
way to write a graphics program that can be ported between
machines easily. You can make a program portable between
different versions of C on the IBM PC by using IBM BIOS
routines rather than the routines described above. Interrupt
0x10 contains a few simple routines. Function 0x0 changes
the graphics mode, for example. Function 0xC will plot a single dot on the screen (see Appendix C for a more complete
description).

The graphics capabilities of the ROM BIOS are very limited. The BIOS routines will only plot a single dot at a time.
You must create your own line- or circle-drawing routines.
This is the price that you pay for portability. Figure 27-6 contains a simple line-drawing routine.

Figure 27-6. dot.c

```
}

#include <dos.h>

plot(x,y,color)
int x,y,color;
{
        _CX = x;
        _DX = y;
        _BH = 0xC;
        _BL = color;
        _AX = _BX;
        geninterrupt(0x10);
}

line(x1,y1,x2,y2,color)
int x1,y1,x2,y2;
{
        int tmp,midx,midy,snx,sny;
```

```
        if(x1 == x2 && y1 == y2)
                plot(x1,y1,color);
        else
        {
                midx = x1 + (x2 - x1)/2;
                midy = y1 + (y2 - y1)/2;
                plot(midx,midy,color);
                if(x1 > x2)
                        snx = 1;
                else
                        snx = -1;
                if(y1 > y2)
                        sny = 1;
                else
                        sny = -1;
                if(abs(x1-midx) > 1 || abs(y1-midy) > 1)
                        line(x1,y1,midx+snx,midy+sny,color);
                if(abs(x2-midx) > 1 || abs(y2-midy) > 1)
                        line(midx-snx,midy-sny,x2,y2,color);
        }
}

main()
{
        _BL = 0x4;
        _BH = 0x00;

        _AX = _BX;

        geninterrupt(0x10);

        {
                int i;
                for(i=0;i<140;i++)
                        plot(10+i,10,1);
        }

        line(10,130,250,30,2);

        getch();
        _BL = 0x3;
        _BH = 0x00;

        _AX = _BX;

        geninterrupt(0x10);
}
```

This program uses only two BIOS functions. Function 0 of interrupt 0x10 is used to change first to graphics mode and then back to text before the program exits. The plot function is built around function 0xC of interrupt 0x10 which is used to draw single dots on the screen.

Direct Memory Graphics

With some graphics adapters, you can write directly to the graphics screen the same way you can write to the text screen. Depending on the number of colors available in a graphics mode, one bit, or set of bits, will represent a single pixel on the screen. By setting or clearing these bits, you can control which pixels will appear on and off.

While this is possible, it's not recommended. Because of the varieties of cards available, with no standard as to the memory configuration, any program written in this manner will be tied to the graphics adapter upon which it was developed. Both the *Turbo C* graphics library and the IBM BIOS automatically account for differences in adapters. There is no reason not to take advantage of these tools.

Text Graphics

The *Turbo C* graphics library also allows you to manipulate text more easily on the IBM screen. Functions exist that allow you manipulate text attributes and draw at any location without building your own direct memory routines or using DOS or BIOS calls.

The main output routines are cprintf( ), cputs( ), putch( ), and getche( ). Any text sent to the screen with these four functions will use all special attributes set with *Turbo C* graphics functions. For example, the function textcolor( ) takes a foreground color as a parameter. All text subsequently printed with the above functions will be printed in that color.

textcolor(GREEN);
cprintf("This text is in green! \n");

You can use gotoxy( ) to place text at any location on the screen. This function takes two int parameters—an *x* and a *y* coordinate. It then will place the cursor at this location. For example, the text in Figure 27-7 will print a message at the upper left corner of the screen without appearing to move the cursor.

Figure 27-7. Using gotoxy( )

```
{
    x = wherex( );
    y = wherey( );
    gotoxy(0,0);
    cprintf("The rest of the screen:");
    gotoxy(x,y);
}
```

The most powerful feature of the *Turbo C* text graphics functions is the ability to create windows of text. As with a viewport in graphics, a window restricts text to a certain area of the screen. The window function takes four integers as parameters: the *x* and *y* coordinates of the upper left corner of the window and the *x* and *y* coordinates of the lower right corner of the window. Any text sent to the screen then will be confined to this window. Figure 27-8 contains an example of this.

Figure 27-8. Creating a Window

```
window(1,1,10,10);
cprintf("Note that this text will wrap");
cprintf("Around after only ten characters\n");
```

There are a large number of other text graphics functions, but these all follow the same general format and are available in the *Turbo C* reference manuals.

These graphics functions normally use direct memory accesses to achieve maximum speed. You may, however, want to avoid this for compatibility reasons. Fortunately, *Turbo C* provides an easy way of doing this. The external variable directvideo controls the way text is output. The directvideo variable is normally set to 1, causing output to be sent directly to the screen. Setting this variable to 0 will cause all output to go through the BIOS. Note that standard print functions like printf( ) always use BIOS calls.

This chapter was just an overview of what can be done with the *Turbo C* graphics libraries. All graphics functions use fairly standard calling conventions, so you should have little trouble using any of them.

Chapter 28

The *Turbo C* Integrated Debugger

Any programming project goes through a number of stages from initial design to final completion. The debugging stage is always the most difficult phase to complete, but compiler errors are fairly easy to fix. If you're using a friendly and helpful package like *Turbo C*, you know in most cases exactly where the error occurred, and have a fairly good idea of what the problem is.

The errors of intent are the most frustrating. They allow the program to compile, but when the program is run, it doesn't do quite what you intended. You will often have no idea where in the program the actual error occurs. You only know the results aren't right.

The newest versions of *Turbo C* includes a full debugger with the rest of the integrated environment. This debugger allows you to see into the program as it's running. You can examine the values of variables, and even modify them as the program runs. While it's a very powerful debugger, all commands are fairly straightforward. Note that this is available only in the integrated environment.

The *Turbo C* debugger allows you to do three things:

• Run the program one section at a time
• Force the program to pause at a certain place
• Examine variables in a program

The compiler must be set to store debugging information as it compiles (the default setting). Go to the Debug menu and make sure the Debug Information option is set to *EXE/OBJs*. This ensures that debugging information is stored in the executable file as it compiles. Choosing this option will cause the environment to move through the different debugging options automatically.

If you look at the Run menu in the integrated environment, you will notice that there is more than one way to run a program.

- You can simply run the program as if you were invoking it from the command line, in which case the program will run until it reaches the end of the executable code.
- You can cause the program to pause at a certain point. For example, if you choose the option Go to Cursor, the program will execute until it reaches the line containing the cursor. When this line is reached, you will be returned to the editor and the line on which the cursor is resting will be highlighted in blue.
- The Step Over option will cause a single line in the program to be executed. If that line contains a function call, that function will be executed in its entirety before control is returned.
- The Trace Into option is almost identical to the Step Over option except that if the line contains a function call, control will be returned to you at the function call.

Once the program has paused in its progress, any of the run commands will cause the program to continue. It will begin from the point at which it left off. You could, for example, run a program line by line, using the Trace Into option (alternatively called by pressing F7). If, at any point, you wanted to run the rest of the program, you could choose the Run option (or press Ctrl-F9).

There are two other ways to cause the program to pause while in the integrated environment. At any time, pressing Ctrl-Break will cause the program to pause. Also, you may place special markers called *Breakpoints* in the text. The program will automatically pause whenever it reaches one of these breakpoints, regardless of the command used to run the program.

There are also two ways to examine the value of a variable. When the program pauses, you can choose the Evaluate option from the Debug menu. This will open a window with three fields. Typing any variable name in the top field will cause the value of that variable to be displayed in the second field (more on this later).

You can also cause the program to continuously display the contents of a variable as the program is running. This is done by placing a *watch* on a variable. A special window contains the values of all variables for which watches have been set.

The best way to describe the features of this debugger is to show them in use. This chapter will show a program filled with errors and how the debugger can be used to spot and remove them.

The program in Figure 28-1 is intended to display some simple mathematical values on the screen. First, it should display a number and its square. Then it should again display this square along with that number multiplied by the factorial of five and some other values. Finally, it should display the factorial of nine.

Figure 28-1. errors.c

```
#include <stdio.h>

int squareit(int a)
{
    int b;

    b *= a * a;

    printf("I just squared %d and got %d\n",a,b);
    return;
}

printit(int a,int b,int c,int d,char * name)
{
    printf("a is %d b is %d c is %c d is %d name is %s\n",a,b,c,d,name);
}

int factorial(int num)
{
    int i,total;
```

```
    for(i=0,total=0;i<=num;i++)
        total = i;

    return total;
}

main()
{
    char * name;
    int fac,square,i,b;

    square = squareit(15);
    fac = factorial(5);

    name = "A name";

    printit(square,square * fac,12,31,&name);

    for(i=0;i<=9;i++)
        b *= i;

    printf("'b' is %d\n",b);
}
```

The output this program was intended to display is shown in Figure 28-2.

Figure 28-2. Intended Results From Figure 28-1

I just squared 15 and got 225
a is 225 b is 27,000 c is 12 d is 31 name is A name
'b' is 362,880

This program is filled with bugs, however. If you run it, you will instead get the output shown in Figure 28-3. (Select OS Shell on the menu to see the results. Enter Exit at the command line to return to *Turbo C*.)

Figure 28-3. Actual Results from Figure 28-1

I just squared 15 and got 31275
a is 32 b is 160 c is ♀ d is 31 name is W◇K
'b' is 0

Without a debugger, you would have to painstakingly step through the program yourself, trying to determine where the program is doing something other than what you intended.

The first printf( ) function is wrong. It says the square of 15 is 3126. The best thing to do is check the state of the program when the line is reached. This can be done by setting a breakpoint on the line containing the printf( ) function call. Enter the editor and move the cursor to the line containing this statement (line 9). Now go to the Break/Watch menu and choose the Toggle Breakpoints option. (Ctrl-F8 will do this directly from the editor.) This should cause the line in question to turn green (See Figure 28-4).

Figure 28-4. Screen 1

```
 File    Edit    Run    Compile    Project   Options   Debug    Break/watch
══════════════════════════════════ Edit ══════════════════════════
     Line 9      Col 1    Insert Indent Tab Fill Unindent      S:ERRORS.C
#include <stdio.h>

int squareit(int a)
{
    int b;

    b *= a * a;

    printf("I just squared %d and got %d\n",a,b);
    return;
}

printit(int a,int b,int c,int d,char * name)
{
    printf("a is %d b is %d c is %c d is %d name is %s\n",a,b,c,d,name);
}

int factorial(int num)
────────────────────────────── Message ──────────────────────────
```
F1-Help F5-Zoom F6-Switch F7-Trace F8-Step F9-Make F10-Menu

Now run the program by pressing (Ctrl-F9). The program should come to a halt on that line. Next, you should examine the variables that are causing the error. Go to the evaluate window by pressing Ctrl-F4. Enter the letter *a* and press Enter. This displays the value of *a*, which is 15. So far, this is correct. Check the value of *b*. It's 31275, just as the printf( ) function said. Something must be wrong with the way the value is assigned to *b* in the previous statement. Enter *a * a* in the top field. It evaluates to 225, as it should. Try *b * = a * a*. It returns 31275, the wrong answer. Something must be wrong with the b * = section. As you might have guessed, this should be written $b = a * a$. Evaluate this expression and you will indeed get the correct answer. (Not all of the bugs will be this simple.) Change line 7 to $b = a *$.

As you can see, nearly any expression can be evaluated here. The only exception is that no function calls can be evaluated.

Now remove the breakpoint by moving the cursor to it and pressing Ctrl-F8. Go to the Run menu and choose the Program Reset option. This will cause any run command to start from the beginning. Now run the program. The first line is now correct, but unfortunately many bugs still remain.

The first line shows that the function squareit( ) is performing math in the correct manner but somehow this value is getting lost when the second printf( ) function is reached. Where is it getting lost? There are many possibilities. The best thing to do is step through the program while watching the values in any variables that hold the value which is getting lost.

Go to the Break/Watch menu and choose the Add Watch option. Enter *square* and hit Enter. Press F6. The message *square: undefined symbol 'square'* should appear in the window (no variable is defined until the program is run.) The current value of square will now always appear in this window. Add watches for the variables *a* and *b* also. Press F6 again to return to the enviroment.

Now hit F8 to begin stepping through the program. The blue bar cursor will move to main( ). Hit F8 again and the cursor will move to the first call of the squareit( ) function (See Figure 28-5).

Figure 28-5. Screen 2

```
  File    Edit    Run    Compile    Project   Options   Debug    Break/watch
╔══════════════════════════════════════ Edit ═══════════════════════════════╗
║     Line 34      Col 6     Insert Indent Tab Fill Unindent * S:ERRORS.C     ║
║  int i,total;                                                              ║
║                                                                            ║
║  for(i=0,total=0;i<=num;i++)                                               ║
║     total = i;                                                             ║
║                                                                            ║
║  return total;                                                             ║
║}                                                                           ║
║                                                                            ║
║main()                                                                      ║
║{                                                                           ║
║  char * name;                                                              ║
║  int fac,square,i,b;                                                       ║
║                                                                            ║
║▓▓square = squareit(15);▓▓▓▓▓▓▓▓▓▓▓▓▓▓▓▓▓▓▓▓▓▓▓▓▓▓▓▓▓▓▓▓▓▓▓▓▓▓▓▓▓▓▓▓▓▓▓▓▓▓  ║
║  fac = factorial(5);                                                       ║
╟──────────────────────────────── Watch ────────────────────────────────────╢
║b: -31962                                                                   ║
║ a: Undefined symbol 'a'                                                    ║
║ square: 1210                                                               ║
╚════════════════════════════════════════════════════════════════════════════╝
  F1-Help  F5-Zoom  F6-Switch  F7-Trace  F8-Step  F9-Make  F10-Menu
```

As you can see by the watch, square contains random data. Hitting F8 will cause the statement to be executed, causing the square of 15 to be placed in square. Press F8. According to the watch window, square now contains 30. Obviously, something is going wrong inside the function.

From the Run menu, reset the program to the beginning. Next, move the cursor to the squareit( ) call and choose the Go to Cursor option from the Run menu (by pressing F4). This will cause execution to stop immediately before executing this line. Now choose the Trace Into option from the Run menu (F7) to follow execution into squareit( ). Move through this function line by line with F8, watching the values of a, b, and square. As you can see, a is correctly squared and placed into b (Figure 28-6). The value of b is correct at the print statement, but it isn't being passed to square. Something must be wrong with the return statement. If you look, you will see that no value is being passed. You want to return the squared value, so change line 10 from *return* to *return b*.

Figure 28-6. Screen 3

```
   File   Edit   Run   Compile   Project   Options   Debug   Break/watch
 ══════════════════════════════════ Edit ═══════════════════════════════════
      Line 9      Col 6    Insert Indent Tab Fill Unindent * S:ERRORS.C
 int squareit(int a)
 {
    int b;

    b = a * a;

    printf("I just squared %d and got %d\n",a,b);
    return;
 }

 printit(int a,int b,int c,int d,char * name)
 {
    printf("a is %d b is %d c is %c d is %d name is %s\n",a,b,c,d,name);
 }

 int factorial(int num)
 ─────────────────────────────────── Watch ──────────────────────────────────
 b: 225
  a: 15
  square: Undefined symbol 'square'
```

F1-Help F5-Zoom F6-Switch F7-Trace F8-Step F9-Make F10-Menu

Now reset and run the entire program. The first part of the second line should now be correct. The second value, 1125, is still wrong, however. This value is square * fac. It is fairly certain that square is correct so you should center your attention on the variable fac. The factorial of five is 120, not five. Obviously something is going wrong with the function call on line 35. Pause the program after this line, either by stepping through the program or by setting a breakpoint, and examine the value of fac. It is five, which is the wrong answer. Something must be happening before this.

Perhaps something is wrong with the return statement for factorial( ). Reset the program, and run until this statement is reached. The value to be returned is in the local variable total. Display this. The variable total is also 5, the wrong answer. The error must occur before this.

The loop on line 22 looks like a likely culprit. Add watches for the two involved variables, total and i. Reset the program and the run to the beginning of the loop. Next, step through the loop using F8, checking the values of total and i on each iteration. They are always off by one. The variable total should be keeping a running total; instead, it is just saving old values of i. The line *total* = *i* should instead be *total* * = *i*. Make this change, reset the program and again step through the loop.

Now total is cleared to 0 and never changes. Because the loop starts at 0, the first multiplication causes total to be cleared to 0. Any further multiplication of total can only result in 0. Perhaps the loop should begin with 1. Change line 22 from

for(i = 0,total = 0;

to

for(i = 1,total = 1;

and rerun the program. Now the second value on the second line is correct.

On to the next error. The third value should be easy. You are just sending a number to a function to be printed. Set a breakpoint on the line in which this value is printed (line 15) and run the program. Evaluate c. It's 12, just as it should be. Why is it printed wrong? Perhaps it's being printed as the wrong type.

As you know, C will let you print any type in any format. When you evaluate a variable, the debugger automatically displays it in the most reasonable manner. Integers are displayed as numbers and characters as letters, for example. You can perform type conversion in the debugger simply by appending a comma and the output format to the variable name. For example, to display the value of c as a character, enter *c,c* in the evaluate window (The first c is the variable name, the second is the format (character)). Try this. The value of c will be displayed as ♀. This was the character that the program displayed. Sure enough, if you look at the call to printf( ), you will see that c is displayed as a character, not a integer. Change

c is %c

to

c is %d

in line 15 and run the program. This variable is now displayed correctly.

There seems to be a similar problem with the variable name. The print statement displays name as garbage. A quick check of this statement shows that it's displayed as a string. This is correct because the variable is also a string. The error must be something else. Remove all old watches by pressing F6, cursoring to each watch and pressing Del. and add a watch on the variable name. Step through this program one statement at a time. In main( ), this watch displays the contents of the local variable name. This variable is set to *A name* and it is passed to the function printit( ) where it's incorrectly printed. Use F7 to step into the function. As soon as execution enters the function printit( ), the watch begins looking at the local variable name. The value in the global variable name should have been passed into the parameter name, but it wasn't. This parameter contains garbage. Obviously something is wrong with the way the variable was passed.

Indeed there is. The variable name is passed to printit( ) with an &. This returns the address of name, which should not be passed to printit( ). Change

&name

in line 39 to

name

The contents of name should now be passed to printit( ) correctly.

There is one final error. The final factorial appears to be incorrect. A quick look at the for loop reveals why. Like the loop in factorial( ), this loop starts at zero instead of one. Change the 0 in line 42 to a 1 and run the program.

It still gives an incorrect answer. If you add a watch for i and b, the reason will soon become apparent. The value of b soon increases above 32,767, the maximum value for an integer. Simply change the variable b to a long and the program should work fine. (Don't forget to change the %d to a %ld to display the value as a long integer.) Figure 28-7 contains the corrected program.

Figure 28-7. file noerr.c

```
#include <stdio.h>

int squareit(int a)
{
    int b;

    b = a * a;

    printf("I just squared %d and got %d\n",a,b);
    return  b;
}

printit(int a,int b,int c,int d,char * name)
{
    printf("a is %d b is %d c is %d d is %d name is %s\n",a,b,c,d,name);
}

int factorial(int num)
{
    int i,total;

    for(i=1,total=1;i<=num;i++)
        total *= i;

    return total;
}

main()
{
    char * name;
    int fac,square,i;
    long b;


    square = squareit(15);
    fac = factorial(5);

    name = "A name";

    printit(square,square * fac,12,31,name);


    for(i=1,b=1;i<=9;i++)
        b *= i;

    printf("'b' is %ld\n",b);
}
```

As you can see, the debugger can help you find many different types of errors quickly. Because C tends not to warn you about overflows, or about displaying data in a nonsensical manner, such errors can be very hard to track without a debugger.

Watches and Structures

You will often want to watch or evaluate variables that aren't normally displayed in one piece. Structures are a prime example. These can be evaluated just like other variables. When you watch or evaluate a structure, its contents will appear as a comma-separated list enclosed in braces. For example, the structure in Figure 28-8 would be displayed in a watch as shown below.

Figure 28-8. A Structure

struct ship
{
      int Port, Starboard, Bow, Stern;
      float value;
      char * captain;
} Enterprise;

Here is the watch returned from the structure in Figure 28-7:

{ 4, 5, 6, 3, 4.52, "Steve"}

This can be confusing without the names so *Turbo C* also allows you to display a structure with each of the field names. Simply display the variable using r as the format. The watch Enterprise,R might display the values below.

{Port:4, Starboard: 5, Bow:6, Stern:3, Value:4.53, Captain:"Steve"}

Changing Variables

While this chapter does not show an example of it, you can change the value of a variable while the program is paused.

First, display the value in the evaluate window. When the old value appears in the second field, use the Down Arrow key to move the cursor to the bottom field. Enter the value you wish to assign the variable here. You may then resume the program. The value will have been changed to this new value.

The Call Stack

The Call Stack is worth mentioning. Choosing this option will display a window containing the functions currently being executed. For example, while execution is in main( ), the call stack window will contain only *main( )*. If main( ) calls printit( ), the call stack will contain *main( )* and *printit( )* until control returns back to main( ). If printit( ) were to call a function called put_letter( ), the call stack would contain *main( ), printit( )* and *put_letter( )* until control is passed back to *printit( )*. The call stack is mainly useful when you are unsure when a function is getting called or you are unclear of the path taken by the program when it is executed.

The best way to learn how to use the *Turbo C* debugger is to practice with it on your own programs with unknown bugs. You will find that even as you are learning to use it, the debugger eases the elimination of errors from your programs. You will soon wonder how you lived without a debugger.

Chapter 29

Some Final Thoughts

This chapter isn't meant to describe any features of C. Instead, it's an attempt to show some of the decisions that will have to be made as you write applications for your PC. No language is an isolated product, and *Turbo C* is no exception. Your working environment, your goals, and the machine on which you run your programs can all influence the way you write C programs.

One of the most important decisions in a programming project is portability. How portable will you make your code? There's no right answer to this question. Your decision will depend on your situation.

Some people write programs only for personal use. In the extreme case, if you're writing a program that will be used only on a color, 640K AT and you've decided that you'll never use a compiler other than *Turbo C,* portability isn't a concern. Any feature that will help you accomplish your task should be used.

Some people write programs for more widespread use. In the extreme case, if you're writing a program that will be used on systems ranging from the IBM PC to the Apple Macintosh to a DEC VAX 11/780 to an HP 3000, you'll also be compiling your programs using a wide variety of compilers because no single C compiler works on all of these systems. Portability will be a major concern. Only those features that are a part of the official C standard should be used. Any direct access of the internal parts of the machine should be avoided. This means no interrupts, no direct screen writes, and no graphics.

Most people will fall somewhere between these two extremes. It's unlikely that you'll move the program to another system, but it's possible. You must weigh each of the additional features that you wish to use against the cost of rewriting your program when it's moved to another version of C.

There are a few ways to keep this rewriting cost down when the program is being written. Many of these rules are simply good programming style and should be followed even if portability isn't a concern.

You should always confine any nonstandard features to functions. For example, if you want to write directly to the screen, create a function that does this for you. Then, whenever you need to write to the screen, call this function instead of doing the write directly. This makes it far easier to move the program to a system that doesn't allow direct screen access. Instead of changing hundreds of screen accesses throughout the program, you only have to change the function.

The same is true for DOS and BIOS calls. While virtually all systems have some kind of get-time routine, there is no standard at all concerning how it should be called. The IBM's use of interrupts to accomplish these tasks actually is fairly atypical. Usually function calls will be provided to perform these tasks. A look through the *Turbo C* reference guide shows that *Turbo C* includes some such function calls – the gettime( ) function, for example. If a given DOS or BIOS call is duplicated in a *Turbo C* function, the *Turbo C* function should be used. If no such function is present, you should write one, calling the DOS or BIOS routine from within that function. Again, the end result is that only a few functions will need to be modified to take advantage of a different machine.

All functions that use nonstandard or machine-dependent code should be kept in the same file or group of files. This helps centralize the code that must be modified when the program is moved. Most files will compile on the new system without change.

Here and there in this book you've read that the effect of a certain expression could vary between compilers. An example of this is the use of more than one increment operator (+ +) in a single expression. These should be avoided wherever possible in programs that may be ported to another machine. When it comes time to move such programs, it's unlikely that you'll remember that such code exists. The bugs caused by differing interpretations of the same expression can be very hard to catch.

There are also a few language features (not function calls) unique to *Turbo C*. While these are very useful, they can make the job of porting a program to another machine very difficult. For example, while string concatenation is nice, it isn't available on most systems. You'll have to combine any such strings into a single string when the program is moved. Fortunately, such problems will usually produce compiler errors rather than the hard-to-catch bugs that non-standard expressions will cause.

Chapter 8 in the *Turbo C User's Guide* provides a very good reference to differences between *Turbo C* and the two major standard definitions of the C programming language. Originally, the only standard definition of C was that described in *The C Programming Language* by Kernighan and Ritchie. Most implementations of C followed this standard. An industry-wide standard (ANSI) is currently being developed. While it hasn't been completed as yet, it will follow closely the Kernighan and Ritchie standard.

For the most part, *Turbo C* is a superset of these two standards. That is, it contains all of the features of each of these standards and will compile any C programs written under these standards without modification. It's called a *superset* because it includes additional features above and beyond those in standard C.

Microsoft C is the other major version of C for the IBM PC. This version of C also follows the Kernighan and Ritchie standard. It also includes some extra library routines for machine-specific functions. *Turbo C* has its own versions of all of these routines. Thus any program written in Microsoft C version 4.0 and lower should compile with *Turbo C*.

You should also be aware that the DOS and BIOS functions listed at the end of this book may change. Most of these changes will involve additions to the original function set. In addition, many networking systems add their own set of functions to the standard set.

Why is this important? You may decide to install your own interrupt functions. You might, for example, consider expanding the functions available from interrupt 0x21. You might also want to use your own interrupt to perform some action.

This is very dangerous. You could find that your programs won't work under OS/2 because new functions have been added that conflict with your functions. One solution is to use only the user interrupts for such functions. Interrupts 0x60 through 0x6F are guaranteed not to be used by DOS or any other similar product (such as a network). However, some memory-resident programs use these interrupts. Even if you use the user interrupts, you may find that your program conflicts with a commercial memory-resident program.

This is by no means all there is to know about the IBM PC, or about *Turbo C*. This book should allow you to use the information found in any good guide to the internal workings of the PC in your C programs. While this book doesn't describe all the BIOS and DOS calls in detail, it should give you enough knowledge to use the information about the BIOS and DOS calls in the appendices to this book.

Appendices

Appendix A
Operator Precedence

From Highest to Lowest

Name	Operator	Binds to
Group 1 (Highest Precedence)		
Function call	( )	The left
Array access	[ ]	The left
Structure pointer	->	The left
Structure member	.	The left
Group 2		
Logical not	!	The right
Bitwise not	~	The right
Negative (change sign)	−	The right
Positive (leave sign)	+	The right
Pointer access	*	The right
Autoincrement	+ +	The left
Autodecrement	− −	The left
Address of	&	The right
Cast	(type)	The right
Sizeof	sizeof( )	The right
Group 3		
Multiplication	*	The left
Division	/	The left
Modulus	%	The left
Group 4		
Addition	+	The left
Subtraction	−	The left
Group 5		
Shift left	< <	The left
Shift right	> >	The left
Group 6		
Greater than	>	The left
Greater than or equal	> =	The left
Less than	<	The left
Less than or equal	< =	The left

Group 7
Equal	= =	The left
Not equal	! =	The left

Group 8
Bitwise and	&	The left

Group 9
Exclusive or	∧	The left

Group 10
Inclusive or	|	The left

Group 11
Logical and	&&	The left

Group 12
Logical or	||	The left

Group 13
Conditional	? :	The right

Group 14
Assignment	=	The right
Operator assignment	% =, + =, − =, * =, / =, < < =, > > =, & =, ∧ =, | =	The right

Group 15 (Lowest Precedence)
Comma		The left

Operators with higher group numbers have lower precedences. Operators in the same group have the same precedence. If two conflicting operators have the same precedence, then each will preferentially bind to the subexpression to the direction shown (either the right or the left).

Note that parentheses could be considered an operator in "Group 0." Anything inside parentheses is evaluated first, regardless of its normal precedence.

Appendix B
DOS Functions

This appendix contains a list of the important DOS functions. Often, you'll be referred to *Turbo C* functions that perform similar or extended versions of the functions presented here.

Interrupt 21h

Interrupt 21h always takes a function number in the AH register.

Function 00h

Terminates program. See exit( ).

Input Parameters:
AH = 00h
CS = Program segment address

Function 01h

Reads a character from the standard input (usually the keyboard) and echoes it to the screen. This function waits for a keypress if none is available. See getch( ).

Input Parameters:
AH = 01h
Return Values:
AL = Character code (If this code is 00h, another call to this function will return the special character ID.)

Function 02h

Prints a character to the standard output (usually the screen). See putch( ).

Input Parameters:
AH = 02h
DL = Character code

Function 03h

Reads a character from the auxiliary device (usually the first serial port).

Input Parameters:
  AH = 03h
Return values:
  AL = Data read

Function 04h

Writes a character to the auxiliary device (usually the first serial port).

Input Parameters
  AH = 04
  DL = Data to write

Function 05h

Writes a character to the printer device (usually the first parallel port).

Input Parameters:
  AH = 05h
  DL = Data to write

Function 06h

Reads or writes a character to the standard devices without performing any operating system checks (such as the check for Ctrl-C).

Input Parameters:
  AH = 06h
  DL = Character to write (FFh means read a character.)
Return Values:
  None unless FFh was sent to the function.
  If a character was ready to be read:
    Zero Flag is clear
    AL = Character read (If AL = 0, a second call will return the extended character ID.)
  If no character was ready to be read:
    Zero Flag is set

Function 07h

Reads a character without sending it to the screen. Doesn't check for Ctrl-C.

Input Parameters:
  AH = 07h
Return Values:
  AL = Character read (If AL = 0, a second call will return
    the extended character ID.)

Function 08h

Reads a character without sending it to the screen. Checks
for Ctrl-C.

Input Parameters:
  AH = 08h
Return Values:
  AL = Character read (If AL = 0, a second call will return
    the extended character ID.)

Function 09h

Writes a string to the standard output device. See the puts( )
family of functions.

Input Parameters:
  AH = 09h
  DS:DX = A far pointer to the string

Function 0Ah

Reads a string from the standard input device. See the gets( )
family.

Input Parameters:
  AH = 0Ah
  DS:DX = A far pointer to the buffer to store the string in

Function 0Bh

Checks to see if a character is available to be read. Doesn't
actually read the character.

Input Parameters:
  AH = 0Bh
Return Values:
  AL = 00h if no character is available; FFh if a character is
    available

Function 0Ch

Clears the keyboard buffer and calls one of the input functions listed above.

Input Parameters:
  AH = 0Ch
  AL = Function number (01h, 06h, 07h, 08h, or 0Ah)
  If AL = 0Ah:
    DS:DX = A far pointer to an input buffer
Return Values:
  If the function called was not 0Ah:
    AL = Character read
  Otherwise, nothing is returned

Function 0Dh

Flushes all buffers. All data to be written to disk is written immediately. See flushall( ).

Input Parameters:
  AH = 0Dh

Function 0Eh

Sets the default drive.

Input Parameters:
  AH = 0Eh
  DL = Drive code (a = 0, b = 1, c = 2, and so on)
Return values:
  AL = Number of drives in the system

Function 0Fh

Opens a file.

Input Parameters:
  AH = 0Fh
  DS:DX = A far pointer to a File Control Block
Return Values:
  AH = 00h if file opened; FFh if file not found

Additional Information:
An FCB (File Control Block) has the following structure:

Byte 0h = Drive
Bytes 01h–08h = Filename
Bytes 09h–0Bh = File extension
Bytes 0Ch–0Dh = Current block (File pointer)
Bytes 0Eh–0Fh = Record size
Bytes 10h–13h = File size
Bytes 14h–15h = File date
Bytes 16h–17h = File time
Byte 20h = Current record
Bytes 21h–24h = A record number

For any call that uses an FCB, you should either fill in the information known to you (that is, the filename and extension) or use an FCB created by another function.

Function 10h

Closes a file.

Input Parameters:
AH = 10h
DS:DX = A far pointer to a File Control Block. This FCB should have been opened with Function 0Fh.

Return Values:
AL = 00h if file closed
AL = FFh if file not found

Function 11h

Searches for a filename. The question mark (?) and the asterisk (*) may be used as wildcards.

Input Parameters:
AH = 11h
DS:DX = A far pointer to an FCB (File Control Block, see Function 0Fh)

Return Values:
AL = 00h if a matching filename is found
AL = FFh if no such file is found. In addition, the buffer at the current DTA (Disk Transfer Area, see Function 1Ah) will be set up as an unopened file.

Function 12h

Searches for the next match. Should only be called after Function 11h.

Input Parameters:
  AH = 12h
  DS:DX = A far pointer to an FCB (File Control Block, see
    Function 0Fh)

Return Values:
  AL = 00h if another matching filename is found
  AL = FFh if no more files are found
  In addition, the buffer at the current DTA (Disk Transfer
    Area, see Function 1Ah) will be set up as an unopened
    file.

Function 13h

Deletes a file or files.

Input Parameters:
  AH = 13h
  DS:DX = A far pointer to an FCB (File Control Block, see
    Function 0Fh)

Return Values:
  AL = 00h if any files are deleted
  AL = FFh if files could not be deleted or did not exist

Function 14h

Reads a block of data from a file and increments the file pointer.

Input Parameters:
  AH = 14h
  DS:DX = A far pointer to an FCB (File Control Block, see
    Function 0Fh)

Return Values:
  AL = 00h if successful; error code if not
  Error codes:

    01h = End of file
    02h = Segment wrap
    03h = Partial record at end of file

Function 15h

Writes a block of data to a file and increments the file pointer.

Input Parameters:
    AH = 15h
    DS:DX = A far pointer to an FCB (File Control Block, see
        Function 0Fh)
Return values:
    AL = 00h if successful; error code if not
    Error codes:

    01h = Disk full
    02h = Segment wrap

Function 16h

Creates a zero-length file, erasing any other file with the same name. Opens the newly created file.

Input Parameters:
    AH = 16h
    DS:DX = A far pointer to an FCB (see Function 0Fh)
Return values:
    AL = 00h if successful
    AL = FFh if not successful

Function 17h

Renames the file.

Input Parameters:
    AH = 17h
    DS:DX = A far pointer to an FCB . The second filename
        should appear here, six bytes after the first in the FCB.
Return values:
    AL = 00h if successful
    AL = FFh if not successful

Function 1Ah

Sets the Disk Transfer Area Address. Can be used with interrupt functions to avoid conflicts with DOS. Should also be used before any of the disk access functions. All disk reads and writes use this area as a buffer.

Input Parameters:
AH = 1Ah
DS:DX = A far pointer to a DTA (usually 128 bytes)

Function 1Bh

Gets information about the default disk drive.

Input parameters:
AH = 1Bh
Return Values:
AL = Number of sectors per cluster
DS:BX = Address of the File Allocation Table
CX = Size of a physical sector in bytes
DX = Number of clusters for the drive

Function 1Ch

Gets information about a drive.

Input parameters:
AH = 1Ch
DL = Drive code (0–26)
Return Values:
AL = Number of sectors per cluster
DS:BX = Address of the File Allocation Table
CX = Size of a physical sector in bytes
DX = Number of clusters for the drive

Function 21h

Reads a selected record. Bytes 21h–24h in the FCB are used to specify the offset to read.

Input parameters:
AH = 21h
DS:DX = A far pointer to an opened FCB
Return Values:
AL = 00h if successful; error code if not
Error codes:
01h = End of file
02h = Segment wrap
03h = Partial record at end of file

Function 22h

Writes a selected record. Bytes 21h–24h in the FCB are used to specify the offset to write.

Input Parameters:
  AH = 22h
  DS:DX = A far pointer to an opened FCB
Return Values:
  AL = 00h if successful, error code if not
  Error codes:
    01h = Disk full
    02h = Segment wrap

Function 23h

Gets the size of a file in records. If successful, the file-size field of the FCB will be updated to the correct size.

Input Parameters:
  AH = 23h
  DS:DX = A far pointer to an unopened FCB
Return Values:
  AL = 00h if file found; FFh if not

Function 24h

Updates the random record field in the FCB to correspond to the file pointer used in sequential reads.

Input Parameters:
  AH = 24h
  DS:DX = A far pointer to an opened FCB

Function 25h

Sets an interrupt vector. See setvect( ).

Input Parameters:
  AH = 25h
  AL = Interrupt number
  DS:DX = A far pointer to the new interrupt handler

Function 26h

Copies the Program Segment Prefix and makes the original one usable by other programs.

Input Parameters:
 AH = 26h
 DX = Segment of the new PSP

Function 27h

Reads a number of records into the DTA (Disk Transfer Area).

Input Parameters:
 AH = 27h
 CX = The number of records to read
 DS:DX = A far pointer to an opened FCB
Return Values:
 AL = 00h if successful, error code if not
 Error codes:
  01h = End of file
  02h = Segment wrap
  03h = Partial record at end of file
 CX = Actual number of records read

Function 28h

Writes a number of records from the DTA (Disk Transfer Area).

Input Parameters:
 AH = 28h
 CX = The number of records to write
 DS:DX = A far pointer to an opened FCB
Return Values:
 AL = 00h if successful; error code if not
 Error codes:
  01h = Disk full
  02h = Segment wrap
 CX = Actual number of records written

Function 29h

Places a filename in an FCB. This will set the appropriate fields in the FCB to the values in a text string.

Input Parameters:
 AH = 29h
 AL, bit 0 = 1 if leading separators are to be scanned off

AL, if bit 1 = 1; the drive ID byte is to be modified only if
a drive is specified in the text string
AL, if bit 2 = 1; the filename will be modified only if the
text string contains a replacement filename
AL, if bit 3 = 1; the filename extension is to be modified
only if a filename extension is specified in the text string
DS:SI = A far pointer to a text string
ES:DI = A far pointer to an FCB

Return Values:
AL = 00h if no wildcards were used
AL = 01h if wildcards were used
AL = FFh if the drive was invalid
DS:SI = A far pointer to the end of the text string
ES:DI = A far pointer to the unopened FCB

Function 2Ah

Gets the system date. See getdate( ).

Input Parameters:
AH = 2Ah
Return Values:
CX = Year: 1980–2099
DH = Month
DL = Day
AL = Day of the week (Sunday = 0)

Function 2Bh

Sets the system date. See setdate( ).

Input Parameters:
AH = 2Bh
CX = Year: 1980–2099
DH = Month
DL = Day
Return Values:
AL = 00h if date set
AL = FFh if date invalid

Function 2Ch

Get the system time. See gettime( ).

Input Parameters:
 AH = 2Ch
Return Values:
 CH = Hour
 CL = Minutes
 DH = Seconds
 DL = Hundredths of seconds

Function 2Dh

Set the system time. See settime( ).

Input Parameters:
 AH = 2Dh
 CH = Hour
 CL = Minutes
 DH = Seconds
 DL = Hundredths of seconds
Return Values:
 AL = 00h if time set
 AL = FFh if time invalid

Function 2Eh

Sets the verify flag. When this flag is set, all disk write operations will perform a read to ensure that data was written successfully.

Input Parameters:
 AH = 2Eh
 AL = 00h to turn the flag off
 AL = 01h to turn the flag on
 DL = 00h

Function 2Fh

Gets the current Disk Transfer Area address.

Input Parameters:
 AH = 2Fh
Return Values:
 ES:BX = A far pointer to the DTA (Disk Transfer Area)

Function 30h

Gets MS-DOS version number.

Input Parameters:
  AH = 30h
Return Values:
  If MS-DOS 1.X
    AL = 00h
  Otherwise
    AH = Major version number
    AL = Minor version number

Function 31h

Terminates and stays resident. Reserves memory and then exits. See keep( ).

Input Parameters:
  AH = 31h
  AL = Exit status
  DX = Memory to reserve in 16-byte paragraphs

Function 33h

Gets or sets the Ctrl-Break flag. If this flag is set, the operating system will check for Ctrl-Break or Ctrl-C.

Input Parameters:
  AH = 33h
  AL = 00h if getting flag status
  AL = 01h if setting flag status
  DL = 00h if turning flag off
  DL = 01h if turning flag on
Return Values:
  DL = 00h if flag is off
  DL = 01h if flag is on

Function 35h

Gets interrupt vector. Returns a far pointer to an interrupt handler. See getvect( ).

Input Parameters:
  AH = 35h
  AL = Interrupt number
Return Values:
  ES:BX = A far pointer to the interrupt handler

Function 36h

Gets free disk space.

Input Parameters:
AH = 36h
DL = Drive code (0–26)

Return Values:
AX = FFFFh if drive invalid; otherwise, contains sectors
per cluster
BX = Available clusters
CX = Bytes per sector
DX = Clusters per drive

Function 38h

Sets or gets country information.

Input Parameters:
AH = 38h
If getting country information:
AL = 00h
DS:DX = A far pointer to a 33-byte buffer
BX = Country code

If setting country information
AL = 01h
BX = Country code

Return Values:
Carry Flag Set if there was an error; clear otherwise
AX = 02h if invalid country code
BX = Country code

Additional Information:
The buffer will be filled as follows:
Bytes 0–1 = Date format:
00h = mm/dd/yy
01h = dd/mm/yy
02h = yy/mm/dd
Bytes 2–6 = Currency symbol string ($)
Byte 7 = Thousands separator (1,000)
Byte 9 = Decimal separator (1.00)

Byte 11 = Date separator (8/8/88)
Byte 13 = Time separator (12:15)
Byte 15 = Currency format
   Bit 1 = spaces between symbol and number
   Bit 2 = 0 if symbol precedes value; 1 if symbol follows value
Byte 16 = Digits after decimal in currency
Byte 17 = 00h if 12-hour clock; 01h if 24-hour clock
Byte 22 = Data list separator

Function 39h

Creates a subdirectory.

Input Parameters:
AH = 39h
DS:DX = A far pointer to a string containing the subdirectory path
Return Values:
Carry flag set if the function failed; clear if it succeeded
AX = 03h if path not found; 05h if access denied

Function 3Ah

Deletes a subdirectory.

Input parameters:
AH = 3Ah
DS:DX = A far pointer to a string containing the subdirectory path
Return Values:
Carry flag set if the function failed; clear if it succeeded
AX = error code
Error codes:
   03h = Path not found
   05h = Access denied
   06h = Current directory

Function 3Bh

Sets the current directory.

Input Parameters:
AH = 3Bh
DS:DX = A far pointer to a string containing the directory path

Return values
   Carry flag set if the function failed; clear if it succeeded
   AX = 3 if the path not found

Function 3Ch

Creates a zero-length file, destroying the file if it exists. See open( ).

Input Parameters:
   AH = 3Ch
   CX = 00h if normal
   CX = 01h if read-only
   CX = 02h if hidden
   CX = 04h if system
   DS:DX = A far pointer to a string containing the filename
Return Values:
   Carry flag set if the function failed; clear if it succeeded
   AX = File handle if successful; error code if it failed
   Error codes:
      03h = Path not found
      04h = No handle available
      05h = Access denied

Function 3Dh

Opens an already existing file. See open( ).

Input Parameters:
   AH = 3Dh
   DS:DX = A far pointer to a string containing the filename
   AL, bit 0–2
      0 if read access
      1 if write access
      2 if read/write access
   AL, bit 3 = 0
   AL, bit 4–6
      0 if compatible with FCBs
      1 if read/write access denied
      2 if write access denied
      3 if read access denied
      4 if full access

AL, bit 7
  0 if file inherited by child processes
  1 if file private to current process

Return Values:
  If function was successful:
    Carry clear
    AX = File handle
  If function failed:
    Carry set
    AX = error code
    Error codes:
      01h = No file sharing
      02h = File not found
      03h = Path not found
      04h = Access denied
      0Ch = Invalid access code

Function 3Eh

Closes a file previously opened with Function 3Dh. See close( ).

Input Parameters:
  AH = 3Eh
  BX = File Handle

Return values:
  The carry flag is set if the function failed; clear if it succeeded
  AX = 06h if the file handle is invalid

Function 3Fh

Reads from a file or device. See read( ).

Input Parameters:
  AH = 3Fh
  BX = File handle
  CX = Number of bytes to read
  DS:DX = A far pointer to the input buffer

Return Values:
  AX = 0h if end of file, otherwise number of bytes read
  The carry flag is set if the function failed; clear if it succeeded

If the function failed:
 AX = 05h if access denied; 06h if invalid handle

Function 40h

Writes to a file or device. See write( ).

Input Parameters:
 AH = 3Fh
 BX = File handle
 CX = Number of bytes to write
 DS:DX = A far pointer to the information to write

Return Values:
 AX = 0h if disk full; otherwise, number of bytes written
 The carry flag is set if the function failed; clear if it succeeded
 If the function failed:
  AX = 05h if access denied; 06h if invalid handle

Function 41h

Deletes a file.

Input Parameters:
 AH = 41h
 DS:DX = A far pointer to a string containing the filename

Return values:
 The carry flag is set if the function failed; clear if it succeeded
 If the function failed:
  AX = 02h if file not found; 05h if access denied

Function 42h

Moves the current file pointer. See lseek( ).

Input Parameters:
 AH = 42h
 AL = 00h to move from the beginning of the file
 AL = 01h to move from the current pointer position
 AL = 02h to move from the end of the file
 BX = The file handle
 CX = Top half of the file offset
 DX = Bottom half of the file offset

Return values:
The carry flag is set if the function failed; clear if it succeeded
If the function failed:
AX = 01h if the function number is invalid; 05h if the handle is invalid

Function 43h

Gets or sets file attributes.

Input Parameters:
AH = 43h
AL = 00h if getting the file attribute
AL = 01h if setting the file attribute
CX = The new attribute:
Bit 0 = Read Only
Bit 1 = Hidden
Bit 2 = System
Bit 5 = Archive
DS:DX = A far pointer to a string containing the filename
Return Values:
If getting attribute:
CX = attribute
The carry flag is set if the function failed; clear if it succeeded
If the function failed:
AX = error code
Error codes:
01h = The function number is invalid
02h = The file not found
03h = The path not found
05h = Attribute can't be changed

Function 45h

Duplicates a file handle returned by an open call (Function 3Dh).

Input Parameters:
AH = 45h
BX = The file handle

Return Values:
   AX = A new file handle
   The carry flag is set if the function failed; clear if it suc-
      ceeded
   If the function failed:
      AX = 04h if no handle available; 06h if invalid handle

Function 46h

Forces one handle to point to the same file as another.

Input Parameters:
   AH = 46h
   BX = The first handle
   CX = The handle to be changed
Return Values:
   The carry flag is set if the function failed; clear if it suc-
      ceeded
   If the function failed:
      AX = 04h if no handle available; 06h if invalid handle

Function 47h

Gets the current directory.

Input Parameters:
   AH = 47h
   DL = The drive code (0–26)
   DS:DX = A 64-byte buffer in which to place the path
Return Values:
   The carry flag is set if the function failed; clear if it suc-
      ceeded
   AX = 0Fh if the drive is invalid

Function 48h

Allocates a block of memory. Will only work from memory-
resident programs and .COM files. Note that this is not the
same as any of the malloc( ) function.

Input Parameters:
   AH = 48h
   BX = Number of paragraphs of memory to reserve

Return Values:
  If the function succeeded:
    Carry flag is clear
    AX = Segment of allocated block (offset is 0)
  If the function failed:
    Carry flag is set
    AX = 08h if insufficient memory
    BX = size of largest available block

Function 49h

Releases a memory block obtained through Function 48h.

Input Parameters:
  AH = 49h
  ES = Segment of the previously allocated block
Return Values:
  The carry flag is set if the function failed; clear if it succeeded
  If the function failed:
    AX = 09h if the segment is invalid

Function 4Ah

Changes the size of a memory block obtained through Function 4Ah.

Input Parameters:
  AH = 4Ah
  BX = The new size of the block
  ES = Segment of the previously allocated block
Return Values:
  The carry flag is set if the function failed; clear if it succeeded
  If the function failed:
    AX = 08h if insufficient memory; 09h if the segment is invalid
    BX = size of largest available block

Function 4Bh

Executes a program.

Input Parameters:
  AH = 4Bh

AL = 00h if executing a program, 03h if executing an over-
lay
ES:BX = A far pointer to a parameter block
DS:DX = A far pointer to the program specification
Return Values:
The carry flag is set if the function failed; clear if it succeeded
All registers are destroyed if the function succeeds; otherwise:
AX = error code
Error codes:
01h if function invalid
02h if file not found
05h if access denied
08h if insufficient memory
0Ah if environment invalid
0Bh if format invalid

Function 4Ch

Terminates with return code. Exits the program and sends
the return code to MS-DOS.

Input Parameters:
AH = 4Ch
AL = Return code

Function 4Dh

Gets the return code of a program run with Function 4Bh.

Input Parameters:
AH = 4Dh
Return Values:
AH = 00 if normal termination
AH = 01 if terminated with Ctrl-C
AH = 02 if terminated by a critical error
AH = 03 if terminated with Function 31h
AL = return code

Function 4Eh

Searches for a file.

Input Parameters:
AH = 4Eh
CX = Attribute to use in the search
DS:DX = A far pointer to a character string containing the filename (may contain wildcards)
Return Values:
If successful:
Carry flag is clear
In the DTA (Disk Transfer Area):
Byte 21 = Attribute
Bytes 22–23 = File time
Bytes 24–25 = File date
Bytes 26–29 = File size
Bytes 30–42 = Filename
If unsuccessful:
Carry flag is set
AH = 02h if path invalid; 12h if no matching entry found

Function 4Fh

Searches for the next match. This function should only be called after calling Function 4Eh.

Input Parameters:

AH = 4Fh
Return values:
See Function 4Eh.

Function 56h

Renames a file.

Input Parameters:
AH = 56h
DS:DX = A far pointer to a character string containing the old name
ES:DI = A far pointer to a character string containing the new name
Return Values:
The carry flag is set if the function failed; clear if it succeeded

If the function failed:
    AX = 02h if file not found
    AX = 03h if path not found
    AX = 05h if access denied
    AX = 11h if not same drive

Function 57h

Gets or sets file date and time.

Input Parameters:
    AH = 57h
    BX = File Handle
    If getting time and date:
        AL = 00h
    If setting time and date:
        AL = 01h
        CX = Time
        DX = Date
Return Values:
    If getting the time and date:
        CX = Time
        DX = Date
    The carry flag is set if the function failed; clear if it succeeded
    If the function failed:
        AX = 01h if the function code is invalid; 06h if the handle is invalid
Additional Information:
    Times have the following format:
        Bits 00h–04h = Seconds / 2
        Bits 05h–0Ah = Minutes
        Bits 0Bh–0Fh = Hours
    Dates have the following format:
        Bits 00h–04h = Day
        Bits 05h–08h = Month
        Bits 09h–0Fh = Year

Function 5Ah

Creates a file with a unique name.

Input Parameters:
  AH = 5Ah
  CX = 00h if normal attribute
  CX = 01h if read-only
  CX = 02h if hidden
  CX = 04h if system
  DS:DX = A far pointer to a character string containing a
    path specification
Return Values:
  AX = File handle
  DS:DX = A far pointer to a character string containing the
    actual filename
  The carry flag is set if the function failed; clear if it suc-
    ceeded
  If the function failed:
    AX = 03h if the path was not found; 05h if access was
      denied

Function 5Bh

Creates a new file.

Input Parameters:
  AH = 5Bh
  CX = 00h if normal attribute
  CX = 01h if read-only
  CX = 02h if hidden
  CX = 04h if system
  DS:DX = A far pointer to a character string containing a
    file specification
Return Values:
  AX = File handle
  The carry flag is set if the function failed; clear if it suc-
    ceeded
  If the function failed:
    AX = 03h if the path was not found
    AX = 04h if no handle is available
    AX = 05h if access was denied
    AX = 50h if the file already exists

Interrupt 25h

This interrupt will read disk sectors into a specified memory location. Disk sectors must be located sequentially on the disk.

Input Parameters:
 AL = Drive number (0–25)
 CX = Number of sectors to read
 DX = The starting sector number
 ES:BX = The address of the DTA (Disk Transfer Area)
Return Values:
 The carry flag will be set on an error.

Interrupt 26h

This interrupt will write disk sectors into a specified memory location. Disk sectors must be located sequentially on the disk.

Input Parameters:
 AL = Drive number (0–25)
 CX = Number of sectors to write
 DX = The starting sector number
 ES:BX = The address of the DTA (Disk Transfer Area)
Return Values:
 The carry flag will be set on an error.

Interrupt 27h

This interrupt will exit a program, leaving it in memory. The program must occupy less than 64K (it must be in the tiny model).

Input Parameters:
 DX = Offset to the last byte of the program
 CS = The code segment of the program

Appendix C
BIOS Functions

Interrupt 10h

Video services.

Function 00h

Sets the current video mode.

Input Parameters:
  AH = 00h
  AL = Video Mode
Video Modes:
  00h = 40 × 25 black-and-white text
  01h = 40 × 25 color text
  02h = 80 × 25 black-and-white text
  03h = 80 × 25 color text
  04h = 320 × 200 four-color graphics
  05h = 320 × 200 four-color graphics
  06h = 640 × 200 two-color graphics
  07h = 80 × 25 monochrome text
  0Dh = 320 × 200 16-color graphics
  0Eh = 640 × 200 16-color graphics
  0Fh = 640 × 350 monochrome graphics
  10h = 640 × 350 16-color graphics

Function 01h

Sets the shape and size of the cursor.

Input Parameters:
  AH = 01h
  CH = Starting line for the cursor
  CL = Ending line for the cursor

Function 02h

Sets the *x,y* position of the cursor.

Input Parameters:
  AH = 02h
  BH = Text page number (0 for graphics)

DH = *y* coordinate
DL = *x* coordinate

Function 03h

Finds the current shape and position of the cursor.

Input Parameters:
  AH = 03h
  BH = Text page number (0 for graphics)
Return Values:
  CH = Starting line of the cursor
  CL = Ending line of the cursor
  DH = *y* coordinate
  DL = *x* coordinate

Function 04h

Reads the current light-pen position.

Input Parameters:
  AH = 04h
Return Values:
  AH = 00h if pen down
  AH = 01h if pen not down
  CH = Pixel *y* coordinate
  BX = Pixel *x* coordinate
  DH = Character *y* coordinate
  DL = Character *x* coordinate

Function 05h

Sets the active display page. The number of display pages available varies with the graphics mode and the type of display adapter.

Input Parameters:
  AH = 05h
  AL = Page number

Function 06h

Scrolls a portion of the screen up a specified number of lines.

Input Parameters:
  AH = 06h
  AL = Number of lines to scroll (0 erases the window)

BH = Attribute for the new area
CH = *y* coordinate for the top of the window
CL = *x* coordinate for the left side of the window
DH = *y* coordinate for the bottom of the window
DL = *x* coordinate for the right side of the window

Function 07h

Scrolls a portion of the screen down a specified number of lines.

Input Parameters:
AH = 07h
AL = Number of lines to scroll (0 erases the window)
BH = Attribute for the new area
CH = *y* coordinate for the top of the window
CL = *x* coordinate for the left side of the window
DH = *y* coordinate for the bottom of the window
DL = *x* coordinate for the right side of the window

Function 08h

Reads the character and attribute at the current cursor position.

Input Parameters:
AH = 08h
BH = Text page number
Return Values:
AH = Attribute
AL = ASCII character

Function 09h

Writes one or more copies of an attribute and character at the cursor position.

Input Parameters:
AH = 09h
AL = ASCII character
BH = Test page number
BL = Attribute
CX = Number of characters to write

Function 0Ah

Writes one or more copies of a character at the cursor position without affecting the current attribute.

Input Parameters:
AH = 0Ah
AL = ASCII character
BH = Text page number
CX = Number of characters to write

Function 0Bh

Changes one color in the CGA color palette.

Input Parameters:
AH = 0Bh
BH = Color to change (0–3)
BL = Color to set it to (0–15)

Function 0Ch

Write a graphics pixel.

Input Parameters:
AH = 0Ch
AL = Pixel value (range varies with the number of colors)
CX = *x* coordinate
DX = *y* coordinate

Function 0Dh

Reads a graphics pixel.

Input Parameters:
AH = 0Dh
CX = *x* coordinate
DX = *y* coordinate
Return Values:
AL = Pixel value (range varies with the number of colors)

Function 0Eh

Writes text in teletype mode. This causes the cursor to be moved in the appropriate manner.

Input Parameters:
AH = 0Eh

AL = ASCII Character
BH = Text display page
BL = Foreground color of the character

Function 0Fh

Gets the current video mode (see Function 00h).

Input Parameters:
AH = 0Fh
Return Values:
AH = Number of columns
AL = Video mode
BH = Active text page

Function 10h

Sets EGA palette registers.

Input Parameters:
AH = 10h
AL = 00h for palette register
AL = 01h for border color register
AL = 02h for all registers (including border)
AL = 03h for toggling the intensity/blink bit
BH = Color value
BL = Palette register to set or 00h to enable intensity; 01h to enable blinking
ES:DX = A far pointer to the color list (if setting all registers)

Function 13h

Writes a string to the screen.

Input Parameters:
AH = 13h
AL = Mode
Legal modes:
00h = String contains characters only; don't update cursor
01h = String contains characters only; update cursor
02h = String contains both attributes and characters; don't update cursor

03h = String contains both attributes and characters; up-
date cursor
  BH = Text page number
  BL = Attribute (for modes 00h and 01h)
  CX = Length of the string
  DH = *y* coordinate to write the string
  DL = *x* coordinate to write the string
  ES:BP = A far pointer to the string

Interrupt 13h

Floppy disk services.

Function 00h:

Prepares the system for disk I/O.

Input Parameters:
  AH = 00h

Function 01h:

Gets the floppy disk status after a disk operation.

Input Parameters:
  AH = 01h
Return Values:
  AH = Status byte
  Status byte :
    Bit 0 set if illegal disk command
    Bit 1 set if disk write-protected
    Bit 2 set if sector not found
    Bit 3 set if DMA overrun
    Bit 4 set if data read error
    Bit 5 set if controller error
    Bit 6 set if seek failure
    Bit 7 set if disk timed out

Function 02h:

Reads from the floppy disk.

Input Parameters:
  AH = 02h
  AL = Number of sectors to read
  CH = Track number

CL = Sector number
DH = Head number
DL = Drive number
ES:BX = A far pointer to a buffer to read into

Return Values:
If successful:
Carry flag cleared
AH = 00h
AL = number of sectors read
If not successful:
Carry flag set
AH = status byte (see Function 01h)

Function 03h:

Writes to the floppy disk.

Input Parameters:
AH = 03h
AL = Number of sectors to write
CH = Track number
CL = Sector number
DH = Head number
DL = Drive number
ES:BX = A far pointer to a buffer to write from

Return Values:
If successful:
Carry flag cleared
AH = 00h
AL = number of sectors read
If not successful:
Carry flag set
AH = status byte (see Function 01h)

Function 04h

Checks sections of the disk for possible errors.

Input Parameters:
AH = 03h
AL = Number of sectors to verify
CH = Track number
CL = Sector number

DH = Head number

DL = Drive number

Return Values:

If successful:

Carry flag cleared

AH = 00h

AL = Number of sectors read

If not successful:

Carry flag set

AH = Status byte (see Function 01h)

Function 05h

Format a disk track.

Input Parameters:

AH = 05h

ES:BX = A far pointer to an address field list

Interrupt 14h

Serial port services.

Function 00h

Initializes port.

Input Parameters:

AH = 00h

AL, bits 0–1

10 if seven bits

11 if eight bits

AL, bit 2

0 if one stop bit

1 if two stop bits

AL, bits 3–4

00 if no parity

01 if odd parity

11 if even parity

AL, bits 5–7

000 if 110 baud

001 if 150 baud

010 if 300 baud

011 if 600 baud

100 if 1200 baud
101 if 2400 baud
110 if 4800 baud
111 if 9600 baud
DX = port number

Return values:
AH = status byte
Status byte:
Bit 0 set if data ready
Bit 1 set if overrun error
Bit 2 set if parity error
Bit 3 set if framing error
Bit 4 set if break detected
Bit 5 set if hold register empty
Bit 6 set if shift register empty
Bit 7 set if timed out

Function 01h

Writes a character to a port.

Input Values:
AH = 01h
AL = Character to write
DX = Port number
Return Values:
AH = Status byte (see Function 00h)

Function 02h

Reads a character from a port.

Input Values:
AH = 02h
DX = Port number
Return Values:
AH = Status byte
AL = Character read (if successful)

Function 03h

Gets the status of a port.

Input Values:
  AH = 03h
  DX = Port number
Return Values:
  AH = Status byte

Interrupt 16h

Keyboard services

Function 00h

Reads a character from the keyboard; waits if none is ready.

Input Values:
  AH = 00h
Return Values:
  AH = The scan code
  AL = The ASCII character

Function 01h

Checks to see if a character is waiting to be read.

Input Values:
  AH = 01h
Return Values:
  If a character is waiting:
  Zero flag is clear
    AH = The scan code
    AL = The ASCII character
  Otherwise the zero flag is set

Function 02h

Returns the keyboard status variable stored in location 0x417.

Input Values:
  AH = 02h
Return Values:
  AL = Keyboard status variable

Interrupt 17h

Printer services.

Function 00h

Writes a character to the printer.

Input Parameters:
  AH = 00h
  AL = Character to write
  DX = Printer number

Return Values:
  AH = Status byte
  Status byte:
    Bit 0 set if timed out
    Bit 3 set if I/O error
    Bit 4 set if printer selected
    Bit 5 set if out of paper
    Bit 6 set if acknowledge
    Bit 7 set if printer not busy

Function 01h

Initializes a printer port for use and gets its status.

Input Parameters:
  AH = 01h
  DX = Printer number

Return Values:
  AH = status byte (see Function 00h)

Function 02h

Initializes a printer port for use and gets its status.

Input Parameters:
  AH = 02h
  DX = Printer number

Return Values:
  AH = Status byte (see Function 00h)

Appendix D
Values Generated by the Keyboard

Each entry in these tables consists of two entries. The first entry is the character in the first keyboard buffer position. The second entry is the character in the second buffer position. Some BIOS routines return the first entry in the AL register and the second in the AH register. These values were generated by an IBM PC. If you have a different machine, it probably uses different values.

The ASCII value for each character is listed at the end of this appendix.

The Main Keyboard

Key	Normal		Shift		Ctrl		Alt	
Esc		1		1	(none)		(none)	
One	1	2	!	2	(none)		0	120
Two	2	3	@	3	NULL	3	0	121
Three	3	4	#	4	(none)		0	122
Four	4	5	$	5	(none)		0	123
Five	5	6	%	6	(none)		0	124
Six	6	7	∧	7	(none)		0	125
Seven	7	8	&	8	(none)		0	126
Eight	8	9	*	9	RS	9	0	127
Nine	9	10	(	10	(none)		0	128
Zero	0	11	)	11	(none)		0	129
Minus	−	12	_	12	US	12	0	130
Equals	=	13	+	13	(none)		0	131
Backspace	BS	14	BS	14	BS	14	(none)	
Tab	TAB	15	BACKTAB	15	(none)		(none)	
Q	q	16	Q	16	DC1	16	0	16
W	w	17	W	17	ETB	17	0	17
E	e	18	E	18	ENQ	18	0	18
R	r	19	R	19	DC2	19	0	19
T	t	20	T	20	DC4	20	0	20
Y	y	21	Y	21	EM	21	0	21
U	u	22	U	22	NAK	22	0	22
I	i	23	I	23	HT	23	0	23

O	o	24	O	24	SI	24	0	24
P	p	25	P	25	DLE	25	0	25
Left bracket	[	26	{	26	ESC	26	(none)	
Right bracket	]	27	}	27	GS	27	(none)	
Enter	CR	28	CR	28	(none)		(none)	
A	a	30	A	30	SOH	30	0	30
S	s	31	S	31	DC3	31	0	31
D	d	32	D	32	EOT	32	0	32
F	f	33	F	33	ACK	33	0	33
G	g	34	G	34	BEL	34	0	34
H	h	35	H	35	BS	35	0	35
J	j	36	J	36	LF	36	0	36
K	k	37	K	37	VT	37	0	37
L	l	38	L	38	FF	38	0	38
Semicolon	;	39	:	39	(none)		(none)	
Apostrophe	'	40	"	40	(none)		(none)	
Accent	`	41	~	41	(none)		(none)	
Backslash	\	43			43	EM	43	(none)	
Z	z	44	Z	44	SUB	44	0	44
X	x	45	X	45	CAN	45	0	45
C	c	46	C	46	ETX	46	0	46
V	v	47	V	47	SYN	47	0	47
B	b	48	B	48	STX	48	0	48
N	n	49	N	49	SO	49	0	49
M	m	50	M	50	CR	50	0	50
Comma	,	51	‹	51	(none)		(none)	
Period	.	52	›	52	(none)		(none)	
Slash	/	53	?	53	(none)		(none)	
Space	SPACE	57	SPACE	57	SPACE	57	SPACE	57

The Keypad

Key	Num Lock		No Num Lock		Ctrl		Alt
Home	7	71	0	71	0	119	(none)
UpArrow	8	72	0	72	(none)		(none)
PgUp	9	73	0	73	0	132	(none)
PrtSc	*	55	*	55	0	114	(none)
LeftArrow	4	75	0	75	0	115	(none)

Middle	5	76	(none)		(none)		(none)
RightArrow	6	77	0	77	0	116	(none)
Minus	–	74	–	74	(none)		(none)
End	1	79	0	79	0	117	(none)
DownArrow	2	80	0	80	0	118	(none)
PgDn	3	81	0	81	0	119	(none)
Ins	0	82	0	82	(none)		(none)
Del	.	83	0	83	(none)		(none)
Plus	+	78	+	78	(none)		(none)

The Function Keys

Key	Normal		Shift		Ctrl		Alt	
F1	0	59	0	84	0	94	0	104
F2	0	60	0	85	0	95	0	105
F3	0	61	0	86	0	96	0	106
F4	0	62	0	87	0	97	0	107
F5	0	63	0	88	0	98	0	108
F6	0	64	0	89	0	99	0	109
F7	0	65	0	90	0	100	0	110
F8	0	66	0	91	0	101	0	111
F9	0	67	0	92	0	102	0	112
F10	0	68	0	93	0	103	0	113

The ASCII Character Set

Number	Name	Comment
0	NUL	
1	SOH	
2	STX	
3	ETX	(Ctrl-Break)
4	EOT	
5	ENQ	
6	ACK	
7	BEL	(Sounds a bell)
8	BS	(Backspace)
9	HT	

Appendix D

Number	Name	Comment	Number	Name
10	LF	(Linefeed)	48	0
11	VT		49	1
12	FF	(Form Feed)	50	2
13	CR	(Carriage Return)	51	3
14	SO		52	4
15	SI		53	5
16	DLE		54	6
17	DC1		55	7
18	DC2		56	8
19	DC3		57	9
20	DC4		58	:
21	NAK		59	;
22	SYN		60	<
23	ETB		61	=
24	CAN		62	>
25	EM		63	?
26	SUB		64	@
27	ESC		65	A
28	FS		66	B
29	GS		67	C
30	RS		68	D
31	US		69	E
32	SPACE		70	F
33	!		71	G
34	"		72	H
35	#		73	I
36	$		74	J
37	%		75	K
38	&		76	L
39	'		77	M
40	(		78	N
41	)		79	O
42	*		80	P
43	+		81	Q
44	,		82	R
45	−		83	S
46	.		84	T
47	/			

320

Number	Name
85	U
86	V
87	W
88	X
89	Y
90	Z
91	[
92	\
93	]
94	¿
95	—
96	
97	a
98	b
99	c
100	d
101	e
102	f
103	g
104	h
105	i
106	j
107	k
108	l
109	m
110	n
111	o
112	p
113	q
114	r
115	s
116	t
117	u
118	v
119	w
120	x
121	y

Number	Name
122	z
123	{
124		
125	}
126	~
127	DEL

Index

noerr.c program 267
null character 70

object file 97
open( ) function 136
operator precedence list 277–78
optimizing code 93–96
options menu 30
OS/2 132, 143
outtextxy( ) function 248–49

parameters, of functions 58
pointer array 71
pointer operator 69
pointers 69–75
   allocating space for 71
   array names, as 69, 70
   character strings, as 69–70
   far pointers, memory access and
     156
   file pointers, not to be saved 142
   structure names, as 79
   structure pointers 82
pop-up programs 2
portability
   enhancing 271–74
   graphics programs and 251
#pragma compiler directive 122
precedence 20–21
preprocessor 86–91
printer commands 144–47
   macros, and 146–47
printer stream 143
printers 143–47
printer unready 143
printf( ) function 44–46, 70
   clock interrupts and 211
print stream, creating 143–44
project file 111–12
project management 7, 111–17
putchar( ) function 41–42, 43
putch( ) function 253

random access files 136–42
   example program 139–41
   importance of closing 142
read, absolute disk 193
realloc( ) function 72–73
real numbers 11
rectangle( ) function 250

register
   cs (code segment) 149
   ds (data segment) 149–50
   es (extended segment) 150
   keywords 93, 183
   segment 149
   ss (stack segment) 150
   variables 93–94
registers
   cautions in using 185–87
   displaying contents of 236
regs.c program 237–41
relational operators 26–27
return statement 60–61
return value 27–28, 43–44, 58
run option 6

saving programs 6
scanf( ) function 48–50, 69
screen
   array 159
   attribute byte 163–65
   organization 158–59
   output interrupt 225
   accessing directly 159–60
   writing directly to 235
scrolling, keyboard interrupt and
   225
segmented memory management
   149
segment register 149
sequential access modes 129
setcolor( ) function 249
settextjustfy( ) function 249
settextstyle( ) function 249
setvect( ) function 197
shortcuts, assignment operator and
   21
short int variable type 16
signed numbers, bitwise operators
   and 104
sizeof( ) function 67, 68
small model 201
splitting a program between files
   97–98
ss (stack segment) register 150
standard function, calling 42
standard functions, i/o and 41
statement, C 9
static variables 96, 99